Lizards

By Russ Case

D1113620

Karla Austin, *Business Operations Manager*
Nick Clemente, *Special Consultant*
Barbara Kimmel, *Managing Editor*
Jarelle S. Stein, *Editor*
Kendra Strey, *Project Editor*
Cindy Weston, *Interior Design*
Melanie Irwin, *Design Concept*
Honey Winters, *Cover Design*

Library of Congress Cataloging-in-Publication Data

Case, Russ.
  Lizards / by Russ Case.
     p. cm.
  ISBN 1-882770-91-9
  1. Lizards as pets. I. Title.

  SF459.L5C37 2006
  639.3'95—dc22

2005036585

An Imprint of BowTie Press®
3 Burroughs
Irvine, California 92618

Printed and bound in Singapore
10 9 8 7 6 5 4 3 2 1

Contents

Uroplatus gecko

CHAPTER 1

Reptiles as Pets

Compared with other animals, **reptiles** (our scaly friends—snakes, lizards, and turtles) sometimes get a bum rap. Lots of people think reptiles— especially snakes—are slimy and want to bite and squeeze people, and maybe even use their fangs to inject them with poison. So when the time comes to choose a pet, millions of people pick animals that seem friendlier.

Bearded dragon

Take dogs, for example. Dog owners can play and exercise with their pooches, brush their hair, dress them up, and perhaps even enter them in dog shows. There are special dog beaches and parks, where dog owners gather by the dozens. There you see dogs running around, playing, barking, and having a great time. Dogs are loved because they give love back. They may lick people's faces, jump on their owners, and want to be with them all the time.

Reptiles are different. I've never been to a snake beach or a lizard park, where people frolic and play with their scaly pets. Snakes don't jump up and down when their owners come home from school or work. Lizards and turtles don't lick your face to show how much they love you, and I've never seen a lizard riding in a car with its head hanging out the window and tongue flapping in the breeze. This is because pet reptiles aren't as interactive as are dogs and some other pets. A pet lizard or snake may not

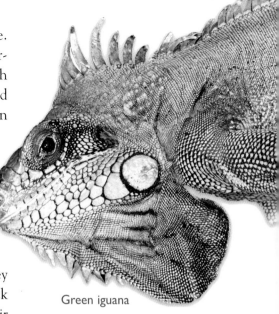

Green iguana

want to be handled all the time, generally won't snuggle with you, and may not respond to your affection (although many will tolerate some handling—when you get to chapter 6, look for the box titled *Lizard Handling Hints*).

Although reptiles are not usually interactive, they still can make great pets–especially for kids!

Collared lizard

Eight Reasons Reptiles Make Great Pets

If your parents are not sure about letting a lizard into your house, ask them to think about the following points:

1. There are some great harmless beginner reptiles.

2. The risk of injury to responsible reptile keepers is much lower than it is with a dog, a cat, or even a parakeet.

3. Compared with other pets, reptiles are low maintenance.

4. Reptiles don't have to be fed every day (but they shouldn't be starved).

5. Their foods are readily available at pet shops and grocery stores.

6. Reptiles aren't hairy, so they make great pets for people with allergies.

7. Keeping reptiles teaches young owners about caring and responsibility.

8. Reptiles are really cool!

Leopard gecko

People Really Like Reptiles

Reptiles have become really popular over the past several years. Go to any pet store—and you'll see what I mean. For one thing, you'll find many different types of **herps**. There are even pet stores that sell only reptiles. You won't find dogs, parakeets, tropical fish, or cats there, but you are likely to see many different types of snakes, lizards (such as iguanas and chameleons), and frogs.

In addition to seeing lots of cool reptiles at pet stores, you'll find oodles of stuff to help you take care of pet herps. Lots of companies sell things that make it easy to provide pet reptiles with happy homes. These things include different types of lights, gizmos to keep your herps warm, branches for them to climb on, cages to keep them in, and bowls for their water and food (you can read more about stuff like this in chapter 4).

People have been keeping pet herps for decades, but within the last ten years the hobby has become really popular. I

Chameleon

can tell you one reason: it is because of the movie *Jurassic Park*. I don't just write books about reptiles. I am also the editor of *Reptiles* magazine, and the fact that the magazine came out about the same time

What's a Herp?

Herp is a nickname for a reptile or an amphibian, and it comes from the word herpetology, which means the study of reptiles and amphibians. A scientist who studies these animals is called a herpetologist.

as *Jurassic Park* was really lucky! People saw the movie and loved it, and as a result, many wanted to learn about reptiles and how to keep them.

> **A pet lizard might be the next best thing to a pet dinosaur!**

Frilled dragon

Something You Should Never Do

Dinosaurs are fascinating. Of course, it's impossible to keep one as a pet (even if you could find one, it would be really expensive to feed it!), but many people think the next best thing to having their own little T-rex is having a pet lizard. And although it's great that so many people became interested in reptiles after seeing *Jurassic Park*, there is a sad side to their new popularity.

After *Jurassic Park*, many pet herps were bought on impulse by people who didn't know how to care for them. People would (and still do) see a neat-looking lizard in a store, and they would buy it right then and there. After all, these animals are very interesting, and some are really colorful. Often, however, the animal would slowly fade away because its new owner didn't know how to take

This baby uromastyx lizard, though small and cute, is likely beyond the care abilities of the average beginner. Never buy a pet lizard on impulse.

care of it. Even today, many reptiles die or end up in animal shelters because of this. That is why you should never buy a pet reptile on impulse!

If you're a smart, caring owner, you'll have a lot of fun with your reptile pets—even though they won't jump up and down when you come home or lick your face. Reptiles are great pets in their own right. Congratulations if you've decided you want to take a shot at keeping them. Now let's take a look at why people like lizards, the reptiles you came here to read about!

Get the Facts First!

Don't purchase any reptile until you have fully researched its housing, feeding, and care requirements—and know how big it will get!

CHAPTER 2

Why People Like Lizards

L izards are extremely popular. Of all the reptiles, they are the ones that most appear to display some personality, and people respond to that. (Snake and turtle owners may not agree with me, of course!) I think lizards pack a lot of personality into their scaly little (and sometimes big) bodies. Why is this?

Bearded dragon

There are several reasons. I think part of it has to do with some lizards' eyes, which look more human than those of some other reptiles. Another reason so many people like to keep lizards as pets is that they come in so many different body shapes and sizes. Lizards, in addition to having many inter-esting body types, can be very pretty. Let's take a closer look.

Chameleon

Lizard Eyes

Let's compare the eyes of snakes and lizards. Snakes' eyes are often (not always) pretty dark, and you can't always tell where they're looking. Plus, they don't have eyelids, so they can't blink or even close their eyes when they're sleeping. Instead of an eyelid, there is a clear scale (called a spectacle) that covers and protects a snake's eye. This makes it look as if a snake's eye is always open, and that "unblinking stare" makes snakes seem kind of alien. Maybe this is one reason some people get the heebie-jeebies

when they're around snakes (another being, of course, that snakes don't have arms or legs).

Some lizards' eyes look a little more like humans'. A healthy lizard's eyes are bright and alert. There is usually a clearly visible pupil, often set against a pretty-colored iris, the colored part around the pupil that changes in size to control the amount of light entering the pupil. And many lizards have eyelids that can cover their eyes, so they can blink and close their eyes when sleeping. (Not all do; the eyes of some

Uroplatus gecko

Looking Lizards in the Eye

The more types of lizards you learn about, the more variety you will see in their behaviors and physical characteristics. Particularly interesting are the different colors and patterns of lizard eyes. Lizards that are mostly active at night typically have slit pupils (like a cat's). This type of pupil can open widely to allow the lizards to see better when it's dark. Lizards that are mostly active during the day usually have round pupils (like a human's) that concentrate light better during daylight. Take a look at the fascinating examples of lizard eyes below:

1. The eye pattern of this Australian spiny-tailed gecko is dizzying.

 2. This Kalahari ground gecko has a slit pupil that opens widely at night to let in light.

3. Shown here is a banded tree anole, a cousin of the green anole you'll read about later.

 4. Chameleon eyeballs are held by moveable bulges that allow these lizards to look in two directions at once!

lizards, including some geckos, are like the eyes of snakes—the eyeballs are covered by spectacles instead of eyelids.) Since you can often tell what a lizard is looking at, it sometimes seems that you know what it's thinking. ("Hey, it's looking at that cricket. I think it's going to go for it!") Plus, sometimes you'll notice that your lizard is looking at you.

Lizard Shapes

Lizards offer a lot of variety when it comes to the shape of their bodies. There are lizards with pointy spines all over their tails and cones on top of their heads. There's even one that looks like a pinecone. Some call it the pinecone lizard, but its real name is shingleback skink. Maybe you'd like to call it by its scientific Latin name, *Trachydosaurus rugosus* (pronounced track-ee-doh-SAURUS roo-GO-sus). Take a look at the box on page 16 to find out more about the shapes of lizard bodies.

Lizards come in many different sizes, too. In Madagascar, an island off the coast of Africa, there are tiny chameleons that are only a couple of inches (about 5 centimeters) long. Meanwhile, if you were to take a boat to Komodo Island, in Indonesia, you might chance upon the Komodo monitor. This is one big lizard—the world's largest—and it can grow to be 10 feet (3 meters) long and weigh about 150 pounds (68 kilograms). A bite from this lizard, also known as the Komodo drag-

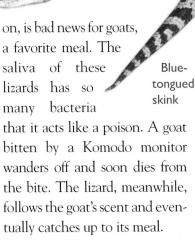

We may look really different, but we're all 100% lizard.

Blue-tongued skink

on, is bad news for goats, a favorite meal. The saliva of these lizards has so many bacteria that it acts like a poison. A goat bitten by a Komodo monitor wanders off and soon dies from the bite. The lizard, meanwhile, follows the goat's scent and eventually catches up to its meal.

As you can see, lizards come in all kinds of shapes and sizes, and some are stranger than others. This is one reason they fascinate people.

Plumed basilisk

A Lizard's Other Name

All living things, including lizards, are known by both common names (such as bearded dragon) and scientific names (in the case of the bearded dragon, *Pogona vitticeps*). Taxonomy is the science used to place animals and plants into categories. Taxonomy, with its use of scientific names, is a very complicated subject, but I'll give you the basics.

Scientific names are typically in Latin, and sometimes they originate from the Greek. *Pogona vitticeps* comes from the Greek word *pogon*, which means beard. Scientific names usually describe the animal.

The two words that make up an animal's Latin name are the genus (first word) and species (second word). The word *Pogona* is the genus name and the word *vitticeps* is the species name. There can be other species within a genus, too. For instance, there's another bearded dragon named *Pogona barbatus*.

Bearded dragon

Did you know that you are a *Homo sapien*? Roughly translated, that means human being. *Homo* is Latin for man and *sapien* is Latin for intelligent. So *Homo sapien* means intelligent man.

Often, animals are named after the people who discover them, and a person's name may be made a part of an animal's scientific name. I know a man named Karl-Heinz Switak. One day, he found a gecko that turned out to be a new species, and later it was named after him: *Coleonyx switaki*.

Your common name most likely means something, too. For instance, my name is Russ, which is short for Russell, which means "red head." Can you guess what color my hair is?

Types of Toes

Lizard feet come in all shapes and sizes. Some geckos, for instance, have paddle-shaped toes that allow them to walk up walls. Chameleons and other tree-dwelling lizards have thick, curled, fingerlike feet that help them grasp branches. Take a look at these funny-looking feet:

The green anole has long toes with thin claws that help it walk along tree branches.

These are the toes of a basilisk, a lizard that can sprint over water without sinking.

A look at the underside of a tokay gecko's foot shows us its padded toes.

Chameleon toes grip branches to steady these lizards in the trees.

Odd Bodies

When looking at the many types of lizards living today, the body parts of lizards vary greatly in size, shape, and function. Consider the differences of the following physical characteristics:

● Eyes: The eyeballs of a chameleon are inside bizarre cone-shaped appendages—think of them as eyeball holders—that stick out from its head. These can swivel around separately from each other, allowing the chameleon's right eye to look in a different direction than its left eye. One can even look forward while the other looks backward.

● Feet: Day and tokay geckos have padded toes shaped kind of like tiny Ping-Pong paddles. On the bottoms of their feet are teeny hairs that enable them to walk on glass or run right up a wall.

● Spines: The spines along the backs of male green iguanas can grow very large and may even flop over. Bearded dragons have soft spines all around their bodies and a spiky, black throat pouch that they can push out, which they may if they're mad.

● Tails: Leopard geckos and African fat-tailed geckos have big heads and bulgy tails. The tails of iguana lizards are longer than the length of the main part of their bodies.

Green iguana

Cool Colors and Pretty Patterns

To some people, the word *pretty* may seem the wrong one to use when talking about reptiles. *Slimy*, *ugly*, and *gross* are words that misinformed people might use. But many reptiles are very pretty—beautiful, even. Many lizards look like they were painted by someone—someone creative, with a great imagination. The beauty of a healthy green iguana showing its bright green coloration, maybe with some blue or orange mixed in; the vivid colors of a panther chameleon (above); and the blazing orange and yellow of some leopard geckos can be astounding. Lizards also

Panther chameleon

A World of Color

Often, a lizard's beautiful color and pattern are what first attract a reptile keeper to a particular species. Some lizards, such as the chameleon, even have the ability to change colors. Some lizards are a plain gray, whereas others sport spotted patterns and carry most of the colors in a rainbow. Look at these amazing lizards:

The fringe-toed lizard has these spots on its head and back.

The tail of this hatchling Standing's day gecko looks like a zebra's—if there were such a thing as a brown and blue zebra.

The shingleback skink gets its name because its scales look like roof shingles.

You're looking at a closeup of the skin of a horned lizard.

Like my spots?
And how about this
yellow collar?

Gecko

show many different patterns. Polka dots, stripes, bands, blotches, and other patterns can be found on lizards in all kinds of combinations—more than you could ever hope to count.

Not every lizard is so pretty, of course. Some are simply brown or gray. But even these less attractively colored and patterned lizards can be interesting to keep and watch.

Can you
see me against
these leaves?

Uroplatus
gecko

Why Do Some Lizards Change Color?

You may know that some lizards can change color. Why do they do this? Maybe you've heard that lizards change color so they can **camouflage** themselves, blending into the background to hide from animals that want to hurt

Diurnal Versus Nocturnal

Diurnal is used to describe animals that are active during the day. The opposite, used to describe animals that are active at night, is **nocturnal**.

them. Camouflage is one reason lizards are colored the way they are, but color changes are often based on mood and the needs of the lizard's body.

Reptiles are **ectotherms**, or **cold-blooded**, which means their body temperature goes up and down depending on the temperature of their environment. If it's hot outside, their body temperature goes up; if it's cold, their

Color Phases

You've already learned that some lizards carry special colors that camouflage them in their surroundings. All lizards change color to some degree. Chameleons are an extreme example; they change colors in response to environmental factors (such as a reaction to a change in temperature) and as expressions of emotions (such as fear). Other lizards may display only slight changes in color. A lizard's dark color phase occurs when the lizard is cold. This deep shade helps the animal absorb warmth from the sun or artificial light. When the lizard heats up, its body color lightens. As an example, look at the following pictures of a uromastyx lizard:

← Shown here in a light phase, this African uromastyx displays a much brighter pattern than when it is cool, as shown below.

Here, the lizard has taken on a dark color, which absorbs the sun to warm the animal up. →

body temperature goes down. Bearded dragons and other **diurnal** (pronounced di-ER-nuhl) lizards may be a darker color when they're cold and a lighter color when they're warm. When they're dark, their bodies absorb heat from the sun faster. As their bodies heat up, they lighten up in color, too.

Some male lizards display bright colors to get the attention of female lizards. They may turn a different color and puff out a colorful throat pouch to attract a female lizard.

Breeding Lizards for Color

Some people make a living by breeding reptiles. These professionals spend a lot of time and money trying to breed lizards and other reptiles of unusual colors. It takes much hard work and time for a new color type of lizard, called a **morph**, to be created, and breeders have to keep a lot of written records about animals in their breeding programs. But reptile breeders are very patient. This is one reason there are more different color types of reptiles available for sale today than in the past.

When someone does come up with a new morph, the reptile can sell for really big bucks—thousands of dollars, even. Sometimes a breeder who has bred a new type of animal will hold on to it for a while and use the new morph for future breedings. Then other people will be able to buy one of these unusual "designer" reptiles. For a while, the new types remain very expensive. Eventually, other people may start breeding them, and the more of these morphs that are available, the

What's a Morph?

An animal with a special color or pattern is often called a color morph (pronounced morf). A breeder may take one kind—say an orange-and-white leopard gecko—and breed it with another type—such as a white-and-purplish one—to see what they'll get.

less they cost. It's kind of like when a new video game first hits the market—initially, it is expensive because it's the newest and coolest game out there. But the price drops after a while, after the game isn't as popular anymore.

Bizarre Behavior

Watching lizards eat and run around is fun. They exhibit a variety of interesting behaviors for many different reasons. For instance, did you know some lizards, including the very popular bearded dragon, wave their "arms" (front legs)? Some scientists and hobbyists believe

A Very Long Tongue

Have you ever seen a chameleon eat? It stands very still on a branch, with its funny-looking eyes keeping close watch on any flying bug that might be coming a little too close. As soon as a bug is in range—ZAP—the chameleon's long, sticky tongue comes shooting out of its mouth to snap up the insect. Chameleon tongues can shoot out twice the length of their bodies; you wouldn't think they could reel them back in, but they can, no problemo—especially when there's a tasty fly stuck on the end.

this behavior is a sign that a lizard recognizes another of its species (as if it's waving hello) or is a submissive gesture. There are lizards called basilisks that run so fast on their hind legs that they can run across water without sinking. In Asia, there are lizards with wide expandable flaps of skin on their sides that enable them to glide from tree to tree, thus earning them their common name, gliding lizards.

One of the most bizarre behaviors exhibited by lizards comes from the horned lizards, also known as horny toads. These animals inhabit desert areas throughout the United States. If one of these lizards gets scared by an animal that it thinks is a predator, a horned lizard can squirt blood from its eyes to try to scare the animal away. Now *that's* weird! This sort of behavior—what a lizard does if it's afraid for its life—is called a **defense mechanism**, or

Anole

This leopard gecko's tail has dropped off. It will grow back but won't look as nice.

defense display. There are many kinds, from the horned lizard's blood-squirting ability to the biting behavior of some other lizards.

One of the better-known lizard defense mechanisms is called tail **autotomy** (pronounced ah-TAH-te-mee). This fancy word refers to the ability that some lizards have to separate their tails from their bodies. They do this to distract a predator and avoid being eaten. Let's say a small fence lizard is minding its own business while sunning on a rock when along comes a coyote puppy that wants to eat it. The coyote might start batting the lizard around a bit, and then the lizard drops its tail. The separated tail starts wriggling and writhing around, all by itself. This confuses the coyote, and while it is watching the squirmy tail, the lizard runs to

The Strangest of the Strange

Lizards certainly are interesting to watch. Your pet may scurry around its cage to catch a cricket lunch or jump from branch to branch to reach its favorite lounging spot. Lizards use special behaviors called defensive displays to show when they are scared or feel threatened by a predator. Below are two examples:

When threatened, the frilled dragon expands a flap of skin around its neck.

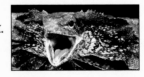

The horned lizard squirts blood from its eyes when it is scared.

After shedding, this web-footed gecko may eat its old skin for a snack.

hide in some bushes or under a rock. Later, the lizard will grow a new tail. This growth process is called **regeneration**.

As if being able to separate a body part weren't odd enough, fish-scaled geckos can twist out of their skins if they need to make an escape. Caught in the jaws of a predator (or the hands of a person), they will squirm and writhe, and their outer layer of skin will actually begin to come off. They may then be able to squirm free, make their escape, and scurry off to wait for their skin to grow back.

Lizards shed their skins as a natural process, not as a defensive behavior. Some, including the popular leopard gecko (you can read about leopard geckos in chapter 6), will eat their own shed skin!

So Why Do You Like Lizards?

These are some of the reasons people are fascinated by lizards. You may like them for the same reasons, or maybe you've got your own. Maybe you like lizards because of their toes or tails or because of the way they look when lying on a branch. There's also the "little dinosaurs" reason I mentioned in chapter 1. Whatever your reasons for liking them, you'll want to know where you can get them. Yes, there's the pet store, of course, but there are other places you can go, too, possibly right in your own backyard.

Plumed basilisk

CHAPTER 3

Where to Get Lizards

We've explored why people like reptiles, particularly lizards. You may be thinking about getting one for yourself. So where do you go to get lizards? Pet stores immediately come to mind. They are where many lizard fans go to get their lizards, and we will get to them in a bit. First, let's go to the source—the place where lizards actually live.

Chameleon

The Great Outdoors

Imagine this: You're hiking along the side of a beautiful mountain stream. You're enjoying the sunshine and having a wonderful time exploring the great outdoors with your friends. A breeze is blowing, the stream is gurgling, and the air smells fresh and clean. You turn a corner and there, **basking** on a rock, is a spiny lizard, a dark gray creature with pointy scales. You stop in your tracks, hush your friends, and approach the lizard as quietly as you can. The lizard remains on its rock, soaking up some welcome rays, and you continue your sneaky approach. The lizard closes its eyes and raises its head slightly, cocking it to one side. You are nearly within grabbing distance. You begin to reach out toward the lizard, and it takes off like a little rocket, running so fast it's hard to tell where it's going as it dashes among some rocks and weeds. You run after it, turn over a few rocks, and dig around the area, but the lizard is

Be Careful!

Be careful about trampling through the wilderness. Always be aware of your surroundings. Never hike in the woods alone. Adults should join in; a fun family outing can be enjoyed by all. Adults can also help you make the right choices about what to wear and take when you go for a hike.

gone. You walk back to your friends, who are laughing.

To anyone who has searched for lizards in nature (also known as the wild), this may be a familiar scene. Of course, the lizard doesn't always get away. Often the result is the successful capture of a wild lizard, and the feeling is great!

Horned lizard

When herping in nature, leave the habitat as you found it. Replace overturned rocks and don't litter.

Hunting for Herps

Many reptile owners started off catching their own pets, long before they began buying them in stores. As a kid, I spent hours searching for herps in the woods near my New Jersey home. I would usually find more amphibians than reptiles, mostly bullfrogs, pickerel frogs, and an occasional salamander.

No matter where you live, some herps are likely to be nearby. They may not be right in your own backyard, especially if you live in a big city with more concrete and buildings

Let Them Sleep!

If you come across a lizard while it's hibernating, leave it alone! It's just rude, and possibly unhealthy for the animals as well, to disturb them while they're hibernating.

Enjoy the beauty of nature while you look for lizards in the wild, but don't destroy anything. Leave everything the way you found it.

than fields and woods, but they may still be found within driving distance. In Alaska, however, you will find amphibians but no wild reptiles—although some sea turtles have been spotted.

Looking for reptiles in the wild is called **herping**, and it's great fun. There are several ways to go about it. The first is to go hiking in a place where you're likely to find some animals. You can usually find lizards by searching woods, desert areas, parks—nearly anywhere that hasn't been bulldozed to make room for houses (although some wild lizards, including geckos and

Can you see why some people use hooks to turn over boards and rocks?

alligator lizards, can often be found around houses in warm climates). Since many lizards lie in the sun, look for places with plenty of basking areas, such as rocks and logs.

Certain times of the year are better to go herping in than others. You won't usually find herps if you look for them during the winter, for instance, especially if you live in an area that gets really cold outside. Remember that lizards are cold-blooded and not very active when they're cool, so

Don't Trespass!

Wherever you go herping, always make sure that you're not trespassing on someone's private property. First get the owner's permission to look for lizards on his or her property. If you just climb a fence or enter a gate, you could find yourself in trouble!

they are not usually moving about during the winter. They're **hibernating**, safely tucked away, while you waste your time stomping about looking for them. Spring, summer, and early fall are usually the best times to have successful herping adventures.

Just as certain times of year are better to look for lizards than others, certain times of day are better, too. Generally, many of the lizards that you would hope to find in the United States are basking lizards, so look for them while the sun is out.

You don't always have to look for lizards in the hot sun, though. Most U.S. geckos,

What Is a Habitat?

A *habitat is the type of land area where an animal lives, such as desert, swamp, or forest.*

for instance, are nocturnal; you have to look for them at night, probably with a flashlight. In Florida, you may not have to go too far to find some geckos. They sometimes gather around people's porch lights at night because they want to eat the flying insects that are attracted to the lights.

What to Take with You

Before you start hiking, get your outdoor herping adventures off to a good start by buying a good reptile field guide. There are several reptile and amphibian field guides readily available in bookstores.

Field guides include photos or drawings (or both) of animals you're likely to find in different areas. The books also provide **range** information, often including

Horned lizard

maps, that tells where the different types of lizards can be found. This will give you an idea of what you may expect to find in a particular type of **habitat** and in a particular part of the country. This type of information is especially useful because some lizards look similar to each other. If you find one and look it up in your field guide, the range information may help you identify it. (Check out the Recommended Reading section at the end of this book for field guide titles.)

Your Herping Kit

If you're hiking outside during the day, you may need insect repellent, sunscreen, water, and other gear standard to hiking. Hats and protective clothing, such as long-sleeved shirts and pants, may be needed. Remember that you may be hiking through wild areas that contain plants with scratchy branches. Wearing short-sleeved shirts and pants could result in cuts and scratches or even sunburn if you forget your sunscreen. Here's a suggested list of what to pack for your day of herping:

☑ Cloth sack
☑ Camera
☑ Field guide
☑ Hiking gear
☑ Insect repellant

☑ Long-handled hook or stick
☑ Protective clothing
☑ Sunscreen
☑ Snacks

It is good to check with someone who is experienced in hiking, such as a knowledgeable clerk at a sporting goods store, to decide exactly what to take with you. What you take often depends on how long you'll be hiking and in what type of area.

There is other stuff you may want to take along on your outing as well. See the box on page 29 for a list.

Some people who look for reptiles in the wild take special long-handled hooks with them, which they use to turn over logs, boards, and other places in which lizards may be hiding.

Don't forget to take a camera! Not everyone who looks for lizards is out to catch them and take them home to keep as pets. Many people like finding lizards in the wild simply to watch them and take pictures. Reptile photography is a fun hobby, and this may be something you would enjoy as well.

Treat Nature with Respect

Whenever you are out in nature, try to disturb things as little as possible. Don't trample and break plants as you hike, and if you turn over any rocks or logs, put them back the way you found them. Never litter—always figure on taking back anything you brought with you into wild areas. There's a saying that's a favorite among nature lovers: Leave nothing but footprints. This means that there should be no sign that you were ever there—no candy wrappers, empty water bottles, broken branches, or disturbed areas. Remember: just because you may not see them doesn't mean animals don't live in these areas, and they would prefer it if their homes (even if they're just rocks) weren't destroyed or pushed over as you pass through their "neighborhoods."

Don't Break Any Laws

It may not be legal where you live to catch wild lizards and take them home. It is illegal to catch some lizards, especially if they are **endangered** and there are not many of that type of lizard left in the wild. Endangered lizards should not be captured for pets.

Sometimes it's best just to take photos of lizards, such as this chuckwalla.

You may need a permit or a fishing license (or both) before you can collect lizards from the wild. So before you head out, check your local laws (you may need to have your parents help you with this), and go about your lizard hunting the legal way. A good place to start your research is by checking your city's government Web sites. You can also check with your local Fish and Game office (Fish and Game is a government organization that enforces laws about fish and animals). Dig around a little, and you'll soon know what you can and can't catch legally.

National parks, which are owned and operated by the government, are beautiful places to observe nature. Some of the most famous national parks in the United States include Yellowstone National Park, in Wyoming, Montana, and Idaho; Yosemite National Park, in California; and Everglades National Park, in Florida. You can find reptiles—and often lots of other animals—in all of these parks. Keep in mind, however, that you are not permitted to capture and take any animal, lizards included, from a national park. These parks are definitely where you are better off just observing and taking pictures of lizards in their natural habitats.

If you ignore laws, you could end up in trouble. At the very least, you'll have to pay a fine if you're caught breaking them. It's always best to be a law-abiding herper.

Pet Stores

Often a pet store is the first place you'll see many different types of lizards. You may even be standing in a pet store reading this right now; and if you look around, you're likely to see some herp cages set up somewhere inside the store and shelves full of reptile supplies. I remember years ago seeing my first desert iguana in a pet store (this lizard is now illegal to sell in California, where I live). Then I saw neat basilisks with big crests on their heads, colorful African flat lizards, and many other unusual and fancy lizards. Up to that point, the only lizards I could ever have hoped to have as a pet were the common fence and alligator lizards I could catch in the hills near my house.

Reptile-only stores usually stock more lizards than other pet stores do.

The better stores can play a big part in your reptile-keeping experiences. Such a store can make all the difference, too, in whether you want to continue keeping lizards. That's a big responsibility, and these pet stores take it seriously. Other stores may be interested only in getting your money, so choose your stores wisely!

Some pet stores sell lots of animals; reptiles may be just one type that you see in such stores. Not far from the reptile section, you may be able to look at puppies, kittens, hamsters, or tropical fish. You may

Don't Buy a Sick One!

Some people buy sick lizards thinking they can help them get well. Don't do it! You're likely to spend a lot of money on veterinary bills and medicine, and there's no guarantee a sick lizard will get well under your care. Why start off with such a problem? Buy only healthy lizards.

The reptile section in a pet store can be a great place to look at lizards.

find many more varieties of reptiles, though, in shops that sell only reptiles, since they usually have more reptiles and more types of reptiles than do the multipet pet shops. The owners of reptile-only stores sometimes breed reptiles, too.

Both types of stores can be excellent places to purchase pet lizards. No matter which type you choose to visit, however, there are some things you should pay attention to. Use the three criteria discussed below when deciding whether to buy a lizard from a store.

Cleanliness

The store and the cages in which the animals are kept should be clean. Cleanliness results in better animal health, whether you're talking about reptiles or giraffes. If you visit a

store and the cages contain rotting, uneaten food or old animal poop—and if the cages stink—then you should think twice about buying any lizards from that store.

The Animals' Health

The animals should be healthy. Common lizard health problems (and how to prevent them) are discussed in chapter 8, but while you're in a store you need to know this stuff, so let's discuss briefly the signs of healthy and sick lizards.

If you see a lizard that's lying on the floor of its cage, and its eyes are sunken and its skin is hanging in loose folds, then it's not healthy. Never buy such a lizard. Healthy lizards are usually plump, especially in the spot

See how this chameleon looks kind of shriveled? It's sick.

Healthy lizards are usually hungry and will often eat in front of you.

where their tails join their bodies. If a lizard's tail, which is where it stores fat, is withered and sunken in, the lizard is not in prime condition.

Sometimes a lizard may look healthy but not actually be healthy. One way to tell if a lizard is healthy is to find out whether it's eating. Ask a store employee to feed the lizard while you watch. If the lizard is not hungry, come back later when it's ready to eat again. If the lizard eats readily, that's a good sign.

A lizard should be alert. If you see one that is looking around, seems interested in its surroundings, and is aware of things, then that's another good sign. A sleeping lizard may not necessarily be ill, but alertness is a sign of health.

If you find a lizard you want to buy, ask to see it close-up. Give it a quick inspection for any parasites (you can read more about them in chapter 8) that may be on it and for stuff coming out of its nose, eyes, or vent (its butt, in other words). There shouldn't be anything stuck to these areas or oozing out of them.

Look also for any wounds, small or otherwise, on the lizard's body. The nose and mouth area can get rubbed raw and become infected if a lizard spends all its time trying to find a way out of its cage. Look for missing scales, broken or missing toes or spines, weird bumps and lumps, and anything else that doesn't look normal. Look in all nooks and crannies of the skin, such as behind the lizards "elbows" and "knees," as these can be areas where parasites gather. While

This gecko has red mites around its eye. Don't buy it!

you're looking at the skin, take notice if it seems to fit the lizard well; if the skin is very loose and hanging off the lizard, leave the animal at the store. A healthy lizard's skin will not be loose along its body, showing lots of wrinkles and folds; it will "fit" the lizard pretty tightly.

It is helpful to know whether an animal was born in captivity or caught in the wild.

Wild-caught lizards may need more time than **captive-bred** lizards to settle down in captivity and may have some health issues that require veterinary care. This doesn't mean a captive-bred lizard comes with a 100 percent health guarantee, but its chances are better. Captive-bred animals are usually more expensive than wild-caught lizards. This is because

Captive-Bred Versus Wild-Caught

Captive-bred lizards can be great choices for several reasons:

- Captive-bred lizards are often healthier and less likely to be infected with parasites.

- Captive-bred lizards are used to captivity, whereas wild-caught lizards are captured in their natural habitats and eventually shipped to pet stores. Lizards that go through this shipping process can be stressed out, which can lead to sickness.

- There are many types of lizards being bred in captivity, including some that make the best pets, such as bearded dragons and leopard geckos.

- By buying captive-bred lizards, you are helping to protect the environment. People worry whenever animals are removed from their habitats to be sold as pets; if too many are taken away, the balance of nature could be affected.

it costs money to raise them in captivity. They are usually healthier than wild animals, and they're also **Bearded dragon** more used to being in captivity and won't typically stress out the way wild animals sometimes will when they're kept in cages. Even though captive-bred lizards cost more, many reptile keepers think the additional price is worth it. See the box on page 35 to learn more about captive-bred lizards versus wild ones.

Not all types of lizards are bred in captivity, however, so if you want a particular type, you may have to get one that was caught in the wild. Wild-caught lizards can still make fine pets.

An alert lizard that doesn't have any skin abnormalities, is

Identifying a Healthy Lizard

Lizards can't talk, so they can't tell you if they're sick. Therefore, it's important that you know what a healthy lizard should look like before you start shopping. Some signs of health problems are easier to see than others. Metabolic bone disease (MBD), something you'll learn more about in chapter 8, is a condition that is caused by nutritional deficiencies and that results in weak bones and deformities. This disease is an example of a health problem that may go unnoticed until the animal is close to death. Never purchase a potentially sick lizard, such as the one shown in the second photo below.

← This is a healthy iguana. Notice the smooth look of the spine.

This iguana has a spinal defect that → may be evidence of MBD.

clean, and is eating is a good choice to buy. It's always a good idea, however, to take any new pet lizard to a veterinarian for a checkup, just to be sure there isn't something wrong inside the lizard.

A Knowledgeable Staff

Do the store employees seem smart, and are they willing to help you even after you get your new lizard home? Some pet store employees work there because they like animals and know a lot about them. Others just need a job. Whenever possible, it's best to find a store with people who know about the animals. And the staff should be willing to help you and answer questions even after

The best stores have lots of different reptile products.

you get your lizard home. Ask ahead of time what the store's policy is regarding this and what kind of guarantee they offer on their animals (in case your new pet gets sick or dies).

Return Guarantees

Many pet stores and some reptile breeders will provide you with another lizard or a credit if something happens to the one you bought within a certain time frame. Ask before you buy.

Green iguana

Some animals escape from their homes, and others are set free on purpose by irresponsible owners who no longer want them. Either situation can be very sad.

Some lost animals end up in animal shelters or rescues, which care for them and try to find them new homes. Sometimes pet owners who can no longer care for their pets, or who no longer want to, will take their animals to these places, hoping the people working at the shelter will find new homes for their pets.

Occasionally, lizards end up at a shelter. Most of these lizards are green iguanas that grew so large their owners couldn't care for them properly. I don't recommend a large green iguana as a first lizard pet, however, or for anyone who doesn't have the ability (including the space for a big cage) to care for it. (For reasons, see the section about green iguanas in chapter 7.)

Sometimes other types of lizards can be found at shelters and rescues, and if you can provide a homeless pet with a new home, that's a great thing. Keep these places in mind if you want a pet lizard (or any other kind of pet), as shelter animals are desperately in need of help. Remember, too, what I said earlier about taking home sick animals. This is usually not a good idea, especially if you're a young herp keeper.

Reptile Breeders and Reptile Expos

Lots of people breed reptiles, and some of them make a lot of money doing so. I don't know about you, but I think this would be a fun job. Some breed only lizards, and others prefer to breed snakes. Some breed lots of different reptiles, including lizards, snakes, and maybe even turtles and frogs. Others may raise only one type of lizard or snake. You can often buy lizards directly from the people who breed them.

Many professional reptile breeders have Web sites you can visit to learn about them and their animals. Some breeders post care tips on their Web sites, and others sell supplies, T-shirts, and other reptile stuff.

Many reptile breeders don't sell their animals to pet stores. They prefer to sell their reptiles either through their Web sites or at reptile shows. These shows, also called expos, usually consist of a number of booths and tables in a big room. There are big expos and small ones; the big ones can attract hundreds of breeders, selling lots of different types of reptiles. Expos pop up all over the world. Currently, the biggest one in the United States takes place each August in Daytona Beach, Florida. Many cities, however, host reptile expos now and then. Some are put together by reptile clubs; others are organized by professional companies. There are European reptile expos, too (Germany has some big ones). You can find listings for upcoming shows in magazines and newspapers as well as on the Internet.

Cool reptile shirts are often for sale at reptile expos.

Some reptile expos feature eye-catching vivarium displays.

This is called a rack system—a common way breeders house their reptiles.

If you've never been to a reptile expo, you really should go. You'll be surrounded by people who like reptiles, and you'll be able to talk to breeders. You will be able to learn a lot at an expo and get a lot of useful information from many people. At some expos, you will be able to sit in on reptile lectures that are given by well-known experts and participate in contests as well as other fun activities. Depending on the show, you may see all types of reptiles for sale, including the latest color morphs (mentioned in chapter 2), as well as old favorites. And there are lots of lizards, of course!

Now that you know where to get your pet lizards and the equipment you'll need to take care of them, we'll take a closer look at the stuff you'll need to keep a healthy, happy lizard.

Buying Reptiles on the Internet

You can often buy pet lizards directly from reptile breeders who have Web sites. Through the Internet, you can locate reptile dealers who may import wild-caught animals that aren't being bred in captivity.

Buying a lizard over the Internet is a bit different from buying one in a pet store. The biggest difference is that you can walk into a pet store and inspect the lizard you want to buy in person. If you find a lizard you want to buy on a Web site, you have to rely on pictures of it and on the word of the breeder to determine whether you really want to get it. Breeders should be patient and willing to offer good care advice and guarantees on their reptiles.

Do some detective work to find out whether an Internet reptile breeder is a good one. You can post questions on the Internet about breeders. You may need someone familiar with Internet chat rooms and message boards to help you. Ask online dealers if they can provide references (the e-mail addresses or phone numbers of people they have previously done business with and had no problems).

CHAPTER 4

Your Lizard's Home

L izards have varying care requirements, so it's important to determine what type of lizard you'll be getting before you purchase all the accessories. Read books and magazines, talk to knowledgeable people (at pet stores, at reptile expos, and in Internet chat rooms), and learn what types of lizards may be best for you (I'll make some suggestions, too, in chapter 6).

Mountain horned dragon

Research is very important. It's advisable to know what a lizard's "hometown" environment was like. Is it a desert lizard or a tropical one? As I've said, knowing how big the lizard will get is very important. Does the lizard drink water from a bowl or by licking droplets off plant leaves? Does it get along with other lizards, or should it be kept by itself? Ask your parents to join in on your research so they can help you get a lizard you will be able to care for. Otherwise they'll have to do all the work! In this chapter, we're going to look at some of the equipment you'll need for your pet. Let's start with its enclosure, the cage—in other words, your lizard's house. It's always best to have your lizard's new home set up before you

Phelsuma gecko

bring your pet home—cozy, ready, and waiting for your pet's arrival. A reptile cage is known by different terms, including **vivarium** and *terrarium*. In this book we use *vivarium*. The type of cage and cage accessories you'll need will depend on the type of lizard you keep.

Cages

Naturally, you need a cage if you want to keep a lizard. You

A nice lizard vivarium such as this simple one can be set up without a huge amount of effort.

This chameleon cage is pretty fancy. The chameleons inside are lucky!

don't want it just running around your house. There are different kinds of cages that are OK to use with lizards. Some are made of plastic, and some of glass. A fish tank can make a fine lizard enclosure, and you can buy these at many places, including pet stores and tropical fish stores.

Those lizard keepers who know how to build stuff make their own cages out of wood and screening. These can be really fancy and may contain live plants, even small trees, as well as the lizards. Cages such as these are often used by people who live in warm areas and want to keep their lizards outside.

For you, I recommend either an aquarium or a cage made especially for reptiles. These are often made of plastic, sometimes with some sort of sliding glass top or front. They also are often available at pet stores and through the Internet.

The size and shape of the cage depend on a few things. For instance, what kind of lizard do you want to get? How big it will get? If you want to keep more than one lizard, can the kind of lizard you want be kept more than one to a cage (some kinds cannot, especially two males)? Does that lizard like to climb? Lizards that like to climb often need tall enclosures. You want to know these things ahead of time so you get the right type of cage. If you get the wrong kind, such as one that's too small, your pet lizard won't be happy.

Room to Grow

A little lizard may not stay little as it gets older. Knowing how big your pet could eventually grow is really important.

A cage that provides some ventilation is important, too. This means that it should allow air to pass through it. Most reptile cages have screened vents built into them for this reason. If you use a fish tank for your lizard's cage, a screen top will help keep the cage ventilated.

In chapter 6, in which I describe some lizards that make good pets for beginner lizard keepers, I'll provide hints about cages that would be good for them. If you want a lizard that I don't mention, read about it elsewhere and learn what you'll need to do to keep it, including how to set up its cage.

Put a Lid on It!

A lid on your lizard cage is always an excellent idea. Even though some lizards are not very good at climbing, they may still manage to escape a lidless cage. So if your lizard cage is an aquarium or other enclosure that has an open top, get a screen top that will fit it snugly. Be sure it's not so loose that your lizard could push against it from below and knock it aside to escape. If that  happens, you might find a dead lizard on your floor or in your closet someday, if you find it at all. Most screen tops come with some type of locking mechanism that will clamp the lid in place. Some sliding screen tops include a locking bolt, too, that prevents the screen from sliding when in the locked position.

Substrate

There are lots of different **substrates** you can get that will work with lizards. There's sand, dirt (with an adult's help, you can bake dirt and sand in the oven to kill off any creepy crawlies that might be hiding in it), bark chips, fake grass (Astroturf), and "reptile carpet," which you can buy at stores that sell reptile supplies. With the Astroturf and reptile carpet, you want to be sure there are no loose strands anywhere on them that could snag your lizard's claws or be eaten by your pet. If you see some, cut them off.

Other substrates include wood chips or shavings of different kinds. Aspen shavings are often used with good results. Avoid cedar shavings, as these can cause some reptiles to get sick. Pine shavings can work, but they are pretty dusty, and your lizard may get sick if it inhales a lot of dust. Pellet substrates are used, too, and some are made of compressed paper. No matter which type of substrate you use, replace it (either in part or completely, if needed) when it becomes wet or soiled. You don't want a stinky cage!

Like the cage, the substrate you use will depend on the type of lizard you get. Some people

The fringe-toed lizard has long toenails that could get snagged on Astroturf or carpeting if you're not careful.

Substrate Options

Newspaper or paper towels are simple solutions to providing a substrate for your lizard's cage. You probably already have these materials around your house. If you want to create a more naturalistic setup for your lizard, consider purchasing one of the following substrate options.

Sand can add a nice touch to a naturalistic cage. You can buy different types, and colors, especially for pet reptiles.

Aspen wood shavings are widely used. They're great odor- and moisture-absorbers.

Bark chips work well for lizards that like humidity. These shavings both absorb moisture and release it.

Astroturf is basically fake grass, and it's an inexpensive substrate that's a bit more attractive than paper. Be sure to keep it clean.

Large pieces of bark and leafy plants offer lizards good hiding places. Along with the artificial grass substrate, they create a natural-looking enclosure

set up their cages to look like the area in which a lizard lived in the wild. For instance, if you live in California and caught a western fence lizard, you might keep it in a cage with a mixture of sand and rocks as a substrate, perhaps with some plants that are native to its home turf. These naturalistic setups can be really eye-catching.

When choosing a substrate, keep this in mind: you don't want one that could hurt your lizard if your pet accidentally ate some of it. Sand, for instance, has been known to cause block-

ages inside reptiles' intestines after they have accidentally eaten it. There are safe sands made especially for reptiles, however, that are digestible. These allow you to have a nice, natural-looking enclosure for your lizards without worrying that they could get sick from eating the sand. You can also help avoid intestinal blockages by putting your lizards' food in a shallow dish that's placed on top of the sand, rather than putting the food on the sand directly. (I'll discuss food in more detail in chapter 5.)

Some lizard keepers keep bare-bones enclosures, with nothing more than paper towel or newspaper in them. These setups may not look as nice as the naturalistic setups, but they are super easy to clean. People who keep their lizards in cages like this usually have many lizards—they may even be professional lizard breeders. Sometimes breeders keep their lizards in plastic containers, stacked together in a rack. If you're a **hobbyist** and simply want to keep some lizards as pets, you will probably want to go with a cage that is nicer and more natural looking. Just remember to keep it clean! Remove any lizard poop and dried up, uneaten food as soon as you see it; don't leave it sitting in the cage for a long time. Daily cleanings are your best bet to keep your lizards healthy.

No matter what type of cage you use, always keep your lizard's habits in mind. If it likes to dig, use a substrate that it can dig in. If it lives in a humid area in the wild, you may need to use bark chips or another substrate that can help keep the cage humid.

Plants look nice, but some lizards may dig them up.

Cage Accessories

Decorations you can put into a lizard cage can be rocks and other objects that make your lizard feel more at home. Rocks are the most popular. Many lizards like to lie on rocks as well as on branches and pieces of logs. Plants, whether they are real or fake, can help make a lizard cage look nicer and can also provide a hiding place for lizards. (See the *Hiding Places Are Important* box on page 50.) If you want to use live plants, just remember you'll have to take care of those, too.

Artificial plants are easier to care for than live ones!

Advanced hobbyists are known to use all kinds of rocks, plants, and branches to set up really fancy cages for their lizards. Some even create waterfalls and pools of water. Maybe this is something you can work up to someday.

Hiding Places Are Important

I know you want to be able to look at your lizard as much as you can. But if you want your lizard to be healthy, you have to provide some places for it to hide while it's in its cage. Lizards need hiding places to feel safe. Remember that they still have some wildness in them, and wild lizards are always on the lookout for things that will hurt them. They also are usually right near somewhere they can run to in case something (such as an animal that may want to eat them) comes after them.

Do your lizard a favor, and provide a hiding place. It can be a piece of bark or a flat rock it could hide under or some plants or a cave. (You can buy ready-made lizard caves at many pet stores.)

Heating and Lighting Equipment

It's ultra-important to make sure your lizard receives the proper type of lighting and is kept warm enough. When you visit a pet store, you'll see all kinds of heating and lighting equipment to help you do this. Again, know what type your lizard will need in order to stay healthy. I'll provide some additional info about this when I discuss specific types of lizards in chapter 6.

Full-spectrum fluorescent lights are very important for diurnal lizards.

Lighting

Some lights are important for your lizards' health. **Ultraviolet (UV) light** gives off invisible rays that lizards absorb into their bodies to help them stay healthy. Having UV light is essential if you want to keep lizards that are active during the daytime. (It's not as important to lizards that are active at night, such as leopard geckos.) You will see all kinds of light tubes that are made for lizards. Read the information on the boxes or have your parents do so, and ask store employees which lights are best for the lizards you want to keep.

Keep in mind that the bulb in a UV light may appear to be functioning even though it eventually stops sending out the UV rays that your lizard needs to stay healthy. So you will need to replace the lights about every six to twelve months, even though they may still light up. Manufacturers often suggest on the packaging when to replace the bulbs.

In addition to providing light, some lamps provide heat. These are called basking lights, and they are usually placed above a rock or a branch or any area a lizard may bask and soak up the heat. For all lizards that are active during the day, I recommend you use both UV and basking lights to help keep your pet in tip-top health.

Lights can be connected to automatic timers that turn on and off by themselves. Set them to go on in the morning and off at night to mimic sunrises and sunsets.

Heating

Lizards can be kept warm several different ways. In addition to overhead fluorescent and basking lights, there are electric heating products, such as heat mats and heat tape, that are placed on the bottom of a

Position basking lamps at one end of the enclosure.

cage. These often come with a **thermostat**, which allows you to set the temperature you want. You can also purchase ceramic heaters.

In chapter 2, we learned that reptiles are cold-blooded, which means that their bodies naturally adjust to the temperature of their environments. Sometimes a lizard needs to reach a certain temperature for its body to perform a particular function such as digestion and egg development. When a lizard's body knows it's time to warm up, it will move to a warmer area. This behavior is called **thermoregulation**.

To help a lizard that's kept in a vivarium to thermoregulate, a responsible reptile keeper places heating and lighting

Not Too Close!

Never place heating or lighting devices where your lizards can come into direct contact with them. Secure the lights on top of the cage's screened lid.

equipment in a way that creates a thermal gradient. The heating elements (such as the heat mat under the tank and the overhead basking light) are placed on one side of the cage to keep that side warm and the other side cooler. By doing this, a lizard is able to position itself where it feels most comfortable. If a lizard is at the end of a cage without the lights and heat, it may feel chilly and move toward the warmer end

I need heat because I'm cold-blooded!

Uroplatus gecko

Keep Your Lizards Warm!

One of the main reasons you need to keep your lizards warm is so they can digest their food. Body heat is necessary to digest food, and because lizards are cold-blooded and don't generate their own body heat, you have to provide the heat for them. If you don't, they won't be able to digest their food, and you'll end up with some very sick lizards.

of the cage. If it begins to feel too hot, it will move back toward the cooler end. This is much better than placing hot lights everywhere and keeping the entire cage the same temperature. (The UV lighting tubes can extend the whole length of the cage since they don't give off much heat.)

Thermometers help you keep the cage the right temperature. (Temperatures are also covered in chapter 6.) Use two—one at the warm end of the cage and one at the cool end.

Step-by-Step Vivarium Setup

The following steps will help you and your parents set up your lizard's cage. These tips apply to any size vivarium. Remember to have the cage set up before you take your pet home!

1. Thoroughly wash the rocks you want to use. Then, place them in the cage and arrange them to your liking. If you are going to be keeping a lizard that likes to bask, place the rock(s) in an area that will be beneath a basking light. Create places for your lizard to hide in so it can feel safe. If you are going to stack rocks, secure them with silicone so they don't topple onto your lizard. Secure rocks to the cage bottom also, so they can't be moved by a digging lizard.

2. Now add clean substrate. Depending on the type of lizard you want to keep, the substrate depth could be from 2 to 4 or so inches (5 to 10 cm).

3. Position any other cage decorations that are to be included such as branches, pieces of driftwood or bark, or logs. Be sure these

are firmly set so the lizard can't move them. If you're using branches, select sturdy ones that can support a lizard. Again, remember to create hiding places (such as large, curved pieces of bark and hollow logs).

4. Position any food and water bowls where you want them. They should be easy for your lizard to find and use. If your lizard eats live crickets, place a small rock or other "island" in the water bowl so crickets that may fall into the water can get out and avoid drowning.

5. Install heating elements and light fixtures. In this chapter, you learned about the importance of providing a thermal gradient. Include a thermometer at each end of the enclosure so you can monitor the temperatures properly at each end of the gradient. Run heating and lighting equipment before you take home your lizard so you know it is operating

properly. It may take a couple days of making minor adjustments to the heating elements in order to maintain the correct temperature.

6. Be sure you have a tight-fitting top for the enclosure.

7. Add lizard(s)!

Paint an Artistic Background

Vivaria that look like a little piece of nature are particularly eye-catching. If you want to get really creative, you could paint a background to attach to your lizard's enclosure. These can look nice if you have a glass cage that you can see through to the back. Here's what you'll need:

☑ Paper or poster board to paint your background on. You could also use anything that you would be able to attach to the back wall of your lizard's enclosure (thin wood, cardboard, butcher's paper, etc.).

☑ Paint and markers or colored pencils. Use a water-based paint. Acrylic paints are available in many different colors and can be washed off with water; you can find them in craft and art stores. Watercolors can look nice, too, either alone or used with acrylics. Use colored pencils or markers—whatever you like to use to create art!

☑ Paint brushes of various sizes

☑ Yardstick

☑ Scissors

☑ Tape

Use the yardstick to measure the back wall of the vivarium, and cut your paper with scissors to fit it. Then paint or draw whatever you like onto your background. You could try to make your painting look like the area where your lizard lived—if

This fancy, three-part setup has its own "painted desert" background. Use it as an inspiration for your artistic vivarium creation!

you're keeping bearded dragons, for instance, you could paint a desert landscape, or if you're keeping a Chinese water dragon, you could paint a tropical-looking background.

Of course, you can paint whatever you want, but natural-looking habitat back-grounds usually look the nicest. Get creative.

Once you're finished and the paint has dried, use the tape to attach your masterpiece to the back of your lizard's enclosure. Sit back and enjoy your artistic efforts!

Humidity

Some tropical lizards, such as day geckos and water dragons (you'll read more about them later), thrive in humid environments so their enclosures should be kept warm and moist. You can provide humidity by lightly misting the cage with water, but not so much that you soak the cage completely. Combined with the heat from lights or other heating devices, the water will create humidity. You can tell if it's humid inside the cage if the walls have moisture (called condensation) on them. Just remember: you want warm and moist; not warm and totally wet!

Food and Water Bowls

Food bowls can be used to hold feeder bugs as well as other lizard foods (see chapter 5 for details about all kinds of feeder bugs and other foods). By using a bowl or a dish (use something your lizard can easily get into and out of) rather than placing food directly on the substrate, you lessen the risk of your pet getting sick by accidentally eating some of the substrate. If you have a lizard that eats fruits and veggies, it's best to

Green water dragon

They don't call me a water dragon for nothing, you know.

With proper lighting, plants usually do well in tropical setups, as shown here, for lizards that like humidity.

use a food bowl. Fruits and veggies are often moist, and substrate can stick to them.

For water, some lizard keepers use shallow bowls; others lightly spray their lizards. If you put a water bowl in the cage, don't be surprised if your lizard uses it as a toilet! Some lizards like to soak in their water bowls. If you do put a water bowl in the cage, make sure it can't be easily tipped over by a lizard climbing into it; you don't want spilled water to soak the cage. If water does spill, replace the wet substrate with dry.

When you visit a pet store, you'll see the equipment mentioned here. There's a ton of reptile-keeping products from which to choose, so decide carefully and with your lizard in mind.

Now that you have an idea of the various things you'll need to keep a lizard, another important bit of info you'll need is about different types of reptile foods. Let's look at those next.

CHAPTER 5

Lizard Food

F eeding pet lizards is usually pretty easy. Every once in a while, though, a lizard won't eat, which could mean it is sick. Sometimes it's just stubborn, and you have to offer different foods to find one that it will eat. Other times it just may not be hungry when you happen to be feeding it, but most healthy lizards are hungry often.

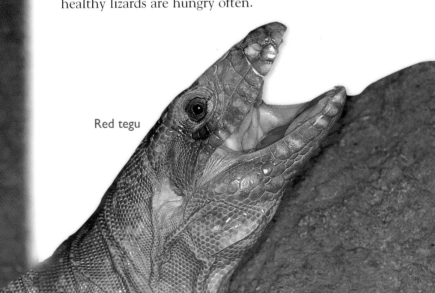

Red tegu

A chameleon's tongue can shoot out so fast you can barely see it. That's bad news for the insect on the receiving end!

Wild lizards eat many different types of foods in nature, but your pet lizards don't have as many choices. They have to eat what you give them. Luckily for them, you have done the necessary research and know ahead of time what types of food to feed your new pets.

In this chapter, I'll review the various foods you may end up feeding your pet lizards. In the next chapter, when I discuss some specific types of

This web-footed gecko is chowing down on a cricket.

Use Supplements!

The foods that captive lizards are fed sometimes lack the correct levels of vitamins and minerals. To make sure your lizards are getting the proper nutrition, add some vitamin-mineral supplements to their foods. This can help prevent diseases that can result from poor nutrition, including some that can cause your lizards' bones to deteriorate. Supplements are available in both liquid and powder forms; discuss them with pet store personnel, and read their labels to determine which types would be best for your lizards.

You can feed lizards "wild" bugs as long as you're sure they haven't been sprayed with any chemicals.

lizards that you may want to keep as pets, I'll also mention the types of foods each eats.

Up first is a type of food some people find a little creepy to feed their animals.

All Kinds of Bugs

Wild **insectivorous** lizards eat many different types of bugs. Whatever they manage to catch, they eat. Life's harder in the wild, and lizards have to make do with whatever they can wrangle up.

Pet lizards generally just need to sit around and wait for their bugs (or other foods) to be dropped into their cages. The trade-off for this convenience is

variety. You are pretty much going to be offering your lizards only a few different types of bugs.

Crickets

Crickets are probably the most popular insect that lizard keepers feed their pets. These bugs are readily available in most pet and reptile stores, and they come in different sizes. There is a cricket size for every lizard, from baby pinhead crickets for dinky baby lizards to adult crickets for bigger lizards.

When you buy crickets at a pet store, the store employee may get them out of a big plastic tub that contains thousands of crickets. You may notice that there are some bumpy, cardboardlike sheets (called egg crates) in these containers and that the employee may bang these against the side of the container. What he's doing is knocking crickets out of their hiding places inside holes in the cardboard. Crickets like to gather there in groups. Once the crickets are knocked loose, the employee will scoop them up and put them in a bag (usually a plastic one that's inflated with air) for you.

Some lizard keepers buy only enough crickets for one lizard feeding. If you do this, also buy a vitamin-mineral supplement (in powder form), and sprinkle some into the bag with the crickets. Then blow some air into the bag, twist the top closed, and shake the bag.

Dust crickets with supplements using a plastic bag.

You'll see that the crickets are now coated with a fine layer of the powder. This is called **dusting**, and it makes the crickets healthier for the lizards to eat because the lizards are also eating the vitamins and minerals that are coating the crickets.

Store-bought crickets are many pet lizards' favorite food.

What Is Insectivorous?

Insectivorous means insect eating. A carnivorous lizard that chows down on crickets, mealworms, and other bugs could also be considered insectivorous.

If you want to make crickets into a really, really healthy food for your lizards, you can **gut load** them. To learn about this, read the *Gut Loading Turns Bugs into Health Food for Lizards* box.

When feeding crickets to lizards, it's best not to put so many bugs into the cage that lots of them find places to hide before your lizards can eat them. Put as many crickets in as your lizards can catch and eat within a few minutes without too many crickets escaping and finding hiding places. Believe it or not, if there are enough crickets, they could end up hurting your lizard. If they get very thirsty, the crickets will be desperate for moisture and may go for the moisture around your lizard's eyes, injuring your pet's eyes in the process. Enough said! It's best to throw in too few crickets, adding more later if necessary, than to toss in too many at once.

You can use a separate empty cage or container in which to feed your lizards, too. If it has no decorations in it, the crickets won't be able to find anywhere to hide. That way, after your lizards eat their fill, you can save the remaining crickets and offer them to your pets at the next feeding.

Keep an eye out for escaped crickets, too. Sometimes it seems no matter how escape-proof you think your lizard cage is, a cricket or two will find some way out of it. I still hear crickets chirping around my house, which I think are descendants of crickets that escaped years ago. Generally, I like the sound of chirping crickets, but sometimes it can drive me crazy, especially if I'm trying to watch TV in the same room!

Cricket Hideouts

When choosing a cage substrate, keep in mind that crickets can sneak down between large pieces of bark or other chunky substrate to hide. You can avoid this by placing only a few crickets in the cage at a time, so the lizards can eat them before the crickets get a chance to hide.

Gut Loading Turns Bugs into Health Food for Lizards

Gut loading crickets and mealworms can make them healthier for your lizards. This means that you feed the bugs healthy foods before feeding the bugs to your lizards. The bugs eat the healthy foods and store the nutrients in their guts. Then your lizards will benefit from these healthy foods when they eat the bugs.

To gut load insects, place them into a plastic container with some fruits and vegetables. Punch some holes in the container's lid, and fit the lid onto the container to seal the bugs in. Let the bugs eat these foods for about a day, and then feed the bugs to your lizards. Some sample gut-loading foods you can feed bugs are apples, carrots, collard and dandelion greens, melons, oranges, yams, potatoes (including peelings), sweet potatoes, and squashes. You can also offer them fish food flakes, dry dog food, and oatmeal flakes. Sprinkle a little reptile vitamin-mineral supplement powder on the crickets' food, too, to make it—and the bugs—extra healthy for your lizards.

Several types of nutrient-packed commercial bug foods (also called chows) that are specially formulated to gut load insects are readily available at pet stores that sell reptiles.

Mealworms

Mealworms are another favorite food of most lizards, and these bugs are sold in most pet stores. Mealworms are actually the **larval** stage of a black beetle. You can buy mealworms in different sizes, just as you can with crickets. There are really little ones for baby lizards all the way up to giant, or king, mealworms for big lizards.

Mealworms bought from a pet store often come in a plastic container that has a type of ground-up cereal that the worms eat. When you open the container, you'll see the cereal, and you may see some mealworms as well. If you don't see any worms right away, you may need to shake up the container a little (put the lid back on before you do this) or dig around in the cereal with your finger until you find some worms.

What Is Larval?

Larval refers to the early part of a bug's life. When a bug is first born, it is called a larva; a caterpillar, for example, is a butterfly or moth larva. Mealworms are the larval stage of the darkling beetle. They'll stay mealworms for about ten weeks before they turn into the beetles.

Worms on Ice

You may not feed all your worms to your lizards at once. You can store leftover mealworms in plastic containers in your refrigerator. Having them in there won't contaminate your food, so don't worry. However, you might have to convince other family members that it's OK to have the worms in the fridge!

Sometimes the pet store just puts the mealworms in a plastic bag.

Mealworms can be gut-loaded just like crickets (again, see the *Gut Loading Turns Bugs into Health Food for Lizards* box). You can also dust them in the same way I described in the cricket section.

Wax Worms

Crickets and mealworms are the most common insects that lizard owners feed their pets, but they're not the only ones.

There are wax worms, for instance. These are bulgy white worms that are kind of wriggly. Like mealworms, wax worms are the larval stage of an insect—in this case, the wax moth. So if you left some around and didn't feed them to your lizard, they would eventually turn into moths (just as mealworms would turn into little black beetles). Wax worms are softer than mealworms, which are skinnier and hard to the touch.

If you have some wax worms in a container, you may be surprised to find silk webbing in the container. Don't worry, this is normal. Wax worms have special glands that produce silk, which the larvae use to walk upon like a tightrope and, when the time comes to turn into moths, to spin their cocoons.

Wax worms are often used to beef up a lizard's weight because these worms have a higher fat

How Often to Feed?

A good way to start is to offer your lizard a few small meals each day rather than one large feeding. A couple of times a day, throw in some crickets or a dish of veggies and you can judge for yourself how often your lizards are interested in eating. If they eat only once a day, feed them once a day. They may even prefer to eat every other day. They'll let you know! One thing to remember, though: if your lizard consistently refuses food over the course of several days, then it may be sick and needs to be taken to the veterinarian.

content. If you have a thin lizard that doesn't seem very healthy, offer it some wax worms and see if it snaps them up.

Other Tasty Bugs

What about the bugs you may find in and around your house? Even in the cleanest of houses, most people find a bug or two crawling around on occasion.

Generally, it's OK to feed bugs you find to your insectivorous lizards. You just need to be sure that the bugs haven't been in contact with any poisons or other dangerous stuff. If you find some beetles in your backyard, they, too, should be pesticide free, and they shouldn't have been in contact with any fertilizers in the grass or garden.

Although some stinging insects may look "meaty," it's best not to offer them to your lizards. This means that bees, wasps, and other dangerous creatures are all off-limits. Generally, you want to stick with bugs that don't have specialized defense mechanisms that could possibly harm your lizards. (Remember when I wrote about defense mechanisms in chapter 2? Well, bugs, just like all animals, have them, too. A wasp that's about to become a meal for a hungry lizard will surely put up a fight and be quick to sting the approaching threat.)

Fruits and Veggies

Many lizards are **carnivorous**— they eat meat, even if it's just bug meat. Others are **omnivorous**— they eat both meat and vegetable matter. There are also **herbivorous** lizards that eat pretty much only fruits and vegetables.

As you now know, getting live insects to feed your lizard is not a problem. Vegetables and fruits are even easier: all you have to do is visit a supermarket or produce stand. Some vegetables are healthier for herbivorous lizards than others are.

As you can see, collared lizards will eat other lizards!

Healthy veggies include bean sprouts; carrots (finely chopped or grated so your lizards don't

Green iguanas

choke on them); collard, mustard, and dandelion greens; green beans; peas; romaine lettuce (never regular iceberg lettuce, which isn't nutritious at all); sweet potatoes; and squashes.

Fruits you can offer omnivorous and herbivorous lizards include apples, bananas, cantaloupes and other melons, figs, kiwis, papayas, peaches, strawberries, and tomatoes.

A salad that combines fruits and vegetables adds variety to your lizard's diet, and variety is a good thing. Offer a few types of foods during one feeding; then offer some different types the

next time. If you feed the same foods over and over, your lizard may get bored and stop eating. There's an old saying, "variety is the spice of life." Well, that goes for lizard food, too!

Remember those vitamin-mineral supplements I mentioned in the bug section? You can sprinkle those over salads as well.

Rodents

You've read about the insectivores and herbivores, but some lizards (big monitors, for instance) eat mice, rats, and possibly small rabbits! I'm not recommending that you get any lizard that gets big

Monitor lizard
(*Varanus sp.*)

Commercial also means manufactured or made by a company. There are different types of commercial reptile diets you can feed your lizard. Some are canned, some are dry, and others are moist and need to be refrigerated. These products can be used to add variety to your lizard's diet, which is very important for maintaining healthy lizards.

enough to eat a rabbit, but some popular smaller pet lizards, including bearded dragons and leopard geckos (both of which you will read about in the next chapter), do eat baby mice. Feeder rodents are readily available at most pet stores, as well as online.

Pinky mice are newborn baby mice. They are called pinkies because they are pink and hairless. Their eyes are not open yet. Unfortunately for them, pinkies can be healthy for some lizards to eat. Their soft bones provide a small amount of calcium, but if they're full of mother's milk, pinky mice are even more beneficial to the lizard because of the calcium contained in the milk. You don't have to dust

pinkies or sprinkle supplements on them, either.

OK, now you know what types of foods you will likely end up feeding your pet lizards. The time has come to learn about some lizards that you should think about getting—those that make great pets, especially for beginners. On to the next chapter!

Don't Overdo Pinkies!

It's not recommended that you feed your lizards too many pinky mice because they're high in fat. Offer them as an occasional treat, as part of your lizards' food rotation.

CHAPTER 6

Five Most Excellent Lizard Pets

When you're looking at lizards in pet stores, at reptile expos, or on Web sites, you're going to notice something: there are lots of different kinds, some are really cool, and you may want to buy them all!

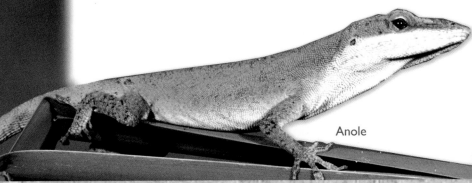

Anole

Most people can't buy every lizard they see, so they have to choose one or two. And this can cause a problem because many beginners (but not just beginners) base their decisions on one thing: they want the most bizarre, coolest-looking lizard. Unfortunately, this is not always a good idea and turns out badly for both the lizard, which may end up dead, and the hobbyist, who will end up disappointed and feeling bad that the lizard died. If it happens to you, you may decide not to keep reptiles at all. That's not good.

To help you avoid such an awful situation, I will now tell you the most important thing to know before you buy a lizard: you need to know how to take care of it and to be able to do so properly. (I said this in chapter 1, but I'm saying it again because it's so important.) Now, I know this seems like a no-brainer, but I'm sad to say that some people who buy the wrong types of lizards act as if they

Leopard gecko

don't have brains! They may see a baby monitor lizard, for instance, and buy it only to find out that their cute little pet is growing into a huge lizard that needs its own room and rabbits to eat. This is one reason lizards (especially big monitors and green iguanas) end up at animal shelters. Only you and your family can decide whether you can care for a particular type of lizard.

Some lizards are easier to care for than others, and if you get one of these, your chances of success will improve. In this chapter, I will discuss some lizards

Bearded dragon

that fit into this category, and I'll also provide some brief care tips for them. This information is meant to get you started; you should still do some research on your own and with your family to make a final decision about which lizard would make the best pet for you.

Bearded dragons such as this one like to bask on rocks.

Bearded Dragons

Bearded dragons are the perfect lizard pet. Healthy ones are hardy and curious, and they are fun to watch. They don't get too big; adults can grow to a maximum of about 2 feet (61 cm), much of which is the tail, and they have pretty golden eyes that make them seem smarter than some other lizards. Many people like bearded dragons because most are mellow enough to be carried around. I've seen bearded dragons left to lie on a branch, seemingly perfectly content to just lounge there and sleep or watch the world go by. At reptile shows, it's not unusual to see them sitting comfortably upon their owners' shoulders.

If you like lizards with spines, you'll like the bearded dragon. Its tan, brown, and white body is covered with

Two-headed reptiles, such as this baby bearded dragon, are fairly rare. If you come across one and it's for sale, count on it being really expensive.

short, pointy-looking spines. (They actually bend, so you won't get poked if you handle the lizard.)

The bearded dragon gets its name because of its beardlike spiky throat pouch, which males puff out during a threat display (to scare off a predator) or to attract a female. The spiny scales on the pouch can turn black during such displays. Females have throat pouches too, but they're not usually displayed as prominently as the males'.

If you keep male and female bearded dragons together, you may see some interesting behaviors. In addition to the throat puffing mentioned above,

females may wave their front legs, and males will bob their heads up and down excitedly. These behaviors may mean different things, including species recognition or submissive behavior. A male that's bobbing his head may be doing so to stake

Bearded dragon

"Buzz off!" this bearded dragon is trying to tell you.

Housing Your Bearded Dragons

A cage should measure at least 30 inches (76 cm) long for a single adult bearded dragon; additional lizards will need additional space. Two could be kept in a 55-gallon (208-liter) aquarium. Young dragons can be kept in smaller enclosures, such as a 10-gallon (38-L) aquarium, but as they grow they will need to be moved to larger quarters. The bigger the cage you can provide, the better, even if you're only keeping one lizard.

out his territory or to attract females. It's his way of saying he's the boss!

Bearded dragons, also called beardies, are easy to find. They are sold in most stores that sell reptiles, and there are always lots of bearded dragons at reptile expos.

Sand makes a good substrate (see chapter 4 for more about sand), and rocks should be provided for the lizards to

Colorful Beardies

Some breeders have specialized in bearded dragons, and as a result you can buy beardies that are yellow, red, and other colors. Keep in mind, though, that lizards that exhibit colors other than the normal tan coloration are more expensive.

lie upon. Remember that these are desert lizards, so a desert landscape should be reproduced in their enclosure.

The bearded dragon originally came from really hot areas in Australia. Therefore, pet bearded dragons need to be kept hot, too. As they're basking lizards, a good basking light is necessary; place the light at one end of the enclosure, above a rock or a branch upon which the lizard can bask. One end of the cage, where the basking light is located, will be hotter (up to 110°F, 43°C) beneath the basking light) than the other end, which should be kept between 80°F and 90°F (27°C and 32°C). This way, the bearded dragon can thermoregulate to stay comfortable. Remember that bearded dragons are diurnal lizards, so they also need UV lighting.

This setup for bearded dragons has climbing sticks and a basking light.

Feeding Your Bearded Dragons

Bearded dragons eat both animal and plant foods. They eat live insects, such as crickets and mealworms—if you want to see a lot of activity in a bearded dragon cage, just drop in a handful of live crickets! Adult bearded dragons eat pinky mice, too. Wax worms can also be offered, but these can be fattening, so don't offer too many.

Feed your dragons a healthy selection of greens, such as collard, dandelion, and mustard greens; veggies, such as romaine lettuce, green beans, and various squashes; and assorted fruits. Be sure all food items are chopped up finely. Place the salad on a dish in the cage, or feed your beardies in a bare cage so they won't accidentally eat sand along with their food.

Vitamin and mineral supplements (including calcium) can be sprinkled on your bearded dragons' food to ensure your lizards are getting the proper nutrition. Follow manufacturer instructions (read the label on the container) if you offer these.

A shallow water dish can be provided, and be sure to keep the water clean, changing it as necessary. You can also mist bearded dragons with water from a plastic spray bottle, such as the type that people use on houseplants. These bottles have adjustable nozzles, so turn it to Mist and spray your bearded dragons. They will drink the water as you spray them.

Leopard Geckos

The leopard gecko is another really popular lizard pet. It's an interesting-looking lizard, too. There are many different kinds of gecko lizards, but the leopard gecko is by far the most popular pet. Normal leopard geckos (meaning those with standard color and pattern) are whitish to cream-colored, with dark purple spots, which is the reason this lizard gets the name leopard gecko. In addition to the normal type, you can buy leopard geckos that have been bred to be bright orange, yellow, white (called the blizzard lizard), or combinations of these colors. So far there aren't any solid purple leopard geckos with red spots,

> **A lot of people like me as a pet!**

Leopard gecko

but who knows what might pop up in the future?

A leopard gecko's tail is kind of weird because it's big and bulbous. In other words, its tail is fat. That's because it stores fat that the lizard can live off of if there's no food available. You have to be very careful of the tail whenever you handle a leopard gecko. Many lizards' tails are autotomous, which, as I explained in chapter 2, means that the tails can break off and grow back. The leopard gecko's tail, however, because of its different shape, can break off very easily

Leopard Gecko Morphs

The leopard gecko is one of the most popular lizards among beginning and advanced keepers alike. One reason is that breeders have had great success in developing beautiful color morphs. The morphs, called designer leopard geckos by some, may display bold yellow and lavender hues and a variety of patterns. Some geckos are striped, some have a combination of stripes and spots, and some are patternless. Take a look at these two stunning leopard gecko morphs:

This high yellow morph is a real eye-catcher. →

← Here is an albino morph. Albino means the animal lacks the ability to produce black pigment.

if the lizard is handled the wrong way. Although the tail regenerates, the new tail never looks as nice as the original. So be very careful whenever you pick up a leopard gecko!

The leopard gecko is one of the lizard species that eats its shed skin. When your leopard geckos begin to shed, you can help them by using a plant mister to moisten their hiding places. Don't spray the shelters so much that the area becomes soaked with water; just enough to lightly moisten them. If you don't provide some moisture at this time, the geckos may have trouble shedding, and some health problems may result.

Leopard gecko

Housing Your Leopard Geckos

The leopard gecko is a nocturnal lizard (active at night). During the day, you may not see your leopard geckos very much. They will most likely spend the daylight hours hiding somewhere in their cage. At night, though, they will come out and patrol their enclosure, hunting for food.

Just because your leopard geckos are active at night doesn't mean you can't watch them. You can buy special nighttime lightbulbs, which are tinted red or blue, and keep these on top of your leopard geckos' cage. Keep them on at night—they will not bother your lizards—and when your geckos come out of hiding, you will be able to watch them exploring their cage.

Cages for leopard geckos don't need to be as big as those for bearded dragons because leopard geckos grow to be only about 6 to 9 inches (15 to 23 cm). A 10-gallon (38-L) aquarium, or a cage of about the same size, is fine for a pair of leopard geckos. Again, big-

This vivarium, with its cool "cutaway rock" (available in some stores) allows you to view the leopard gecko in its daytime hiding spot.

ger is always better, and a 20-gallon (76-L) aquarium can house a few additional geckos.

Place a screen top over your geckos' enclosure to allow fresh air to circulate inside the cage. Plus, it will keep your geckos inside! Leopard geckos aren't known to be great climbers (they can't walk on glass like some other geckos), but why take a risk? Always keep a cover on any lizard cage.

A daytime cage temperature in the mid-80s F (high 20s C) to low 90s F (low 30s C) is good for leopard geckos. You can provide heat by using overhead lights, a heat mat, or heat tape. Put heating devices at one end of the cage, and keep the other end cooler so the lizards can thermoregulate if they walk around during the daytime. The cage can cool down into the 70s F (20s C) at night.

Sand makes a good leopard gecko substrate, as this lizard likes to dig. I recommend that you use the digestible sand I mentioned earlier, but you could use playground sand available at building supply and hardware stores. Bark chips can be used with leopard geckos, too.

Keep a shallow water dish in your leopard geckos' cage, and

clean it frequently. If you don't clean the dish, it will become contaminated with gross fungus and bacteria.

Never keep two male leopard geckos together because they will fight. Keep a male and a female together (you might end up with leopard gecko eggs), or keep only females together. Provide hiding places for them so they'll feel safe. If you don't provide hiding places, your animals could get stressed out and become sick.

Feeding Your Leopard Geckos

Insects are a leopard gecko's favorite food. Remember how I

The African Fat-Tailed Gecko

While you're looking at reptiles, you may see one that looks a lot like the leopard gecko—the African fat-tailed gecko. It has brown-and-tan bands, and some have a white stripe down the back. The fat-tailed gecko doesn't have the prominent spots the leopard gecko does, but the two lizards have a similar body shape.
The fat-tailed gecko's natural habitat is in Africa, where it is hot and humid. This is how its cage should be kept. Using a bark substrate (such as orchid bark), which holds moisture, can help you keep the cage humid.

Care tips for the African fat-tailed gecko are much the same as those for the leopard gecko, so read the leopard gecko section to find out how to care for these guys. Be forewarned, though: African fat-tailed geckos have a reputation for being a bit harder to keep healthy than leopard geckos are.

mentioned that you could add vitamin and mineral powders to insects (by dusting them with the powders) to make the bugs healthier for the lizards? These supplements are a must if you keep a leopard gecko because this lizard doesn't benefit from the healthy rays of ultraviolet lighting described in chapter 4. Can you guess why? Because it's a nocturnal lizard that comes out at night, that's why. The moon doesn't put out the same kind of rays as the sun does!

You can even keep a dish of powdered supplement in your leopard gecko's cage, and the lizard will sometimes eat the powder directly from this dish. Otherwise, you will need to dust the insects you feed to your gecko. Put the insects in a plastic bag, sprinkle some powder into the bag, inflate the bag by breathing some air into it, and shake the bag, mixing the bugs and powder together. Then dump the bugs into the lizard cage. You should notice that they now have a light coating of powder on them.

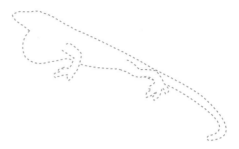

Green Anoles

The green anole is the first pet lizard many reptile keepers, including me, choose. Although it is called the green anole (pronounced a-KNOLL-ee), it is sometimes brown. This is because the green anole can change color. Whether it's green or brown depends on temperature, light, and the lizard's mood. If it's stressed or cold, it could be dark brown (remember that some lizards will darken in color to absorb more heat). If it's healthy and happy, it will be bright green. If your anole is brown all the time and never green, it may be sick.

The male has a pretty purplish throat flap that he usually extends if he's trying to scare off other lizards or to attract a mate. This display is sometimes done at the same

Green anoles are sometimes called chameleons because they can change color. They're not really chameleons, though.

time the lizard is bobbing his head. Females may exhibit a pinkish color on their throats, but they don't have the flaps that males have.

Green anoles are just about the cheapest lizards to buy. If you live in Florida, Georgia, the Carolinas, or another southeastern state, you might be able to catch your own green anoles. I remember the first time I ever saw some wild ones, in North Carolina. I was sitting on an outdoor patio at a restaurant, and there were anoles jumping around on some near-by bushes. Seeing them was really neat because up to then I had seen these lizards only in cages in pet stores.

Housing Your Anoles

Because they don't get big (adult anoles are about 7 inches, 18 cm, long, and they're skinny, too), anoles can be kept in smaller enclosures. Anoles are **arboreal,** which means they like to climb on plants and trees. Arboreal lizards like taller enclosures so they can climb up high, as opposed to ground-dwelling lizards such as bearded dragons and leopard geckos, which need more ground space. No matter what shape the enclosure is, give these lizards branches and leaves (either real or fake) to climb on.

You can keep three or four anoles (don't keep more than one male per cage, though) in a 10-gallon (38-L) aquarium or, better yet, in a cage measuring about 24 inches (61 cm) long by 12 inches (30 cm) deep by 24 inches (61 cm) tall. Add some branches and leafy plants to the cage, and your anole should be very happy. Basking and full-spectrum lights should be provided, too; try to keep the cage temperature during the day somewhere between 75°F (24°C) and 85°F (29°C); it can go down into the 70s F, 20s C, at night.

Feeding Your Anoles

Anoles will eat crickets and mealworms as well as other insects. They eat nectar in the wild, so occasionally you can feed them fruit-flavored baby food. Put it in a small dish, and see if your anoles lap it up.

Chinese Water Dragons

When people want a green lizard, they often get a green iguana. Baby iguanas don't cost too much, and iguanas are really neat looking, especially because of the spines that grow down their backs. However, green iguanas have special care requirements (plus, they will need a huge enclosure once they grow up), so they should not be purchased by first-timers. (I'll discuss iguanas further in chapter 7.)

There is another pretty green lizard that's a better choice for beginners: the Chinese water dragon. This lizard doesn't get anywhere near as big as a green iguana, although some adults can grow to about 3 feet (91 cm), so you will eventually need a pretty big cage (up to 6 feet, 1.8 m, long and a couple of feet tall).

One sad thing about water dragons is they are known for rubbing their noses off while trying to escape their enclosures. They will rub their noses on the cage walls over and over until the skin comes off (see page 109). Their wounds can then become infected. Offering a larger cage may help prevent this behavior. So may taping some paper across the bottom several inches of glass-walled cages (the theory being that if the lizards can't see through the glass, they might not rub their noses against it so much while trying to walk through it).

The Chinese water dragon isn't the only water dragon; there is also the Australian water dragon, which is brown instead of green. The Chinese is a better choice for someone who's just starting out with lizards, though. Besides, they cost less than Australian water dragons.

Housing Your Chinese Water Dragons

Water dragons, like green anoles, like to climb, so their cages (and again, tall cages suit them best) should have plenty of branches. They also need full-spectrum lighting and a thermal gradient, with warm areas and cooler areas in their cages. A good overall cage temperature is in the mid- to high 80s F (high 20s C to low 30s C). Water dragons

Chinese water dragon

can be pretty messy, so be sure their enclosures are kept clean.

You should be able to tell by its name that a water dragon will want water in its enclosure. This lizard is a swimmer, so include a water dish that's big enough to allow your water dragons to go underwater and swim if they feel like it. Your lizards may go to the bathroom in the water so be sure to keep this water dish very clean at all times.

Although your water dragons may want to swim in their water dish, they probably won't drink out of the dish. Use a water bottle to spray water on your lizards, the leaves, the branches in their cage, and the cage walls; you will likely see them drinking up the drops.

Feeding Your Chinese Water Dragons

Water dragons eat the usual bugs that are on an insect-eating lizard's menu; don't forget to gut load crickets and mealworms. Adult water dragons also eat pinky mice. These lizards are omnivorous, so feed them a healthy salad of

Want a groovy green lizard? Try a Chinese water dragon.

chopped-up veggies, too. (See veggie suggestions in the bearded dragon section, as well as in chapter 5.)

Blue-Tongued Skinks

The blue-tongued skink is usually easygoing and tolerates handling better than many other lizards. It's got a thick body and usually grows to a bit over 2 feet (61 cm) in length. The belly is most often whitish; the rest of the body is varying shades of brown, black, and gray, with bands or blotches around the body.

As its name suggests, this lizard has a blue tongue, and it's a

Tongue-Flicking

Lizards (and snakes) will use their tongues to "smell" their environment while looking for food, detecting predators, and searching for mates. A lizard will stick out its tongue, catch scent particles with it, then bring the tongue back into the mouth to rub it against a special sensory organ located there, called the Jacobson's organ.

pretty big tongue at that. You will likely see it flicking in and out of the lizard's mouth. With its short legs, the blue-tongued

A blue-tongued skink hatchling can fit into your hand for a while, but it will get bigger as it grows!

The blue-tongued skink isn't the only lizard with a blue tongue. This is a shingleback skink, a cousin of the blue tongue.

skink is kind of a stumpy-looking lizard. It has smooth scales, too, that make the lizard look shiny. Compare the scales of the blue-tongued skink with the pointier scales of other lizards—called keeled scales—that give their bodies rough and bumpy appearances.

Housing Your Blue-Tongued Skinks

An enclosure equivalent in size to a 55-gallon (208-L) aquarium works well for a single blue tongue. Full-spectrum lights are needed for this lizard. Most blue-tongued skinks (there are different types) are originally from Australia (one type is from Indonesia), and they need temperatures up to 90° F (32°C) during the day. An undertank heater or heat tape can be used to provide heat, as can lights and ceramic heating elements. Blue-tongued skinks aren't known for being climbers; floor space is more important to them, so provide as much as you can.

Feeding Your Blue-Tongued Skinks

This lizard is an omnivore that eats both bugs and veggies. Some people will feed it high-quality dog or cat food to provide protein. Don't give them too much of these foods, however, as poor health can result. You can also give them cooked chicken or turkey.

Even though blue-tongued skinks are pretty mellow lizards, they can still bite. They have big mouths, too, so handle them (and all lizards) with care.

The lizards mentioned in this chapter all make good pets, even for beginners. In the next chapter, I'll briefly discuss some lizards that you may see in pet stores but should wait to own until after you have had more experience keeping lizards.

Blue-tongued skink

I didn't get this fat eating just lettuce, you know!

Lizard Handling Hints

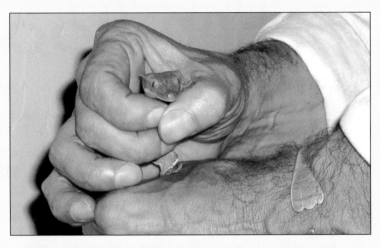

It's hard to resist handling pet lizards. Keep in mind, though, that many lizards don't really like to be handled. Bearded dragons seem to tolerate handling very well, but even a bearded dragon may not always be in the mood to be held.

Lizards are naturally afraid of things that approach them from above. In the wild, predators such as birds often swoop down on them from above, so you can see why a lizard may get scared when your hand is coming down toward it. So when you want to pick up your pet, approach it carefully. Slowly reach into the enclosure and gently grasp the lizard. Pick it up and maintain a firm yet gentle grip, supporting the lizard from below and along the length of its body.

If your lizard begins thrashing around while you're holding it, be careful that you don't accidentally injure it while trying to hold on. The lizard could even hurt itself while struggling, and it's at this time that you could get bitten. If the lizard doesn't calm down, gently put it back in its cage and try again another time.

CHAPTER 7

other Cool Lizards — Just Not for Beginners

You're going to see lots of different lizards when you go to pet stores and reptile expos. In chapter 6, I mentioned five types that make good pets for beginners and gave you some brief care tips. The lizards I'm going to mention in this chapter can make wonderful pets, too, but are best left to people who have been keeping lizards for a while.

Chameleons

The Komodo monitor (also known as the Komodo dragon) is the world's largest lizard. You would never want to be bit by one!

After you've successfully kept some beginner lizards for a while, you can work your way up to the cool lizards in this chapter. Just don't buy them until you're ready for them. Otherwise, problems could occur. And who needs problems? Because I don't recommend that beginners get the lizards I'm going to mention here, I am not going to provide care tips for them. I just want to tell you about them.

Green Iguanas

The green iguana, common in Latin American countries, is one of the most popular lizards in the world. It's a magnificent-looking creature, with its green color, spines along its back, big head scales, and golden eyes. Sadly, the beautiful green iguana

This cute baby green iguana will soon be very, very big.

is also a lizard that suffers a lot because people who buy it find out, too late, that they can't take good care of it. One reason is because while baby "greenies" are cute and can be kept in small cages, they will grow to 6-foot-long (1.8-meter-long) adults that need a lot of room—some green iguana owners keep their lizards in room-size enclosures!

Green iguanas, especially adult males, can be kind of grumpy, too, which can result in owners being whipped by their pets' strong, long tails, or even bitten or badly scratched. A bite from an angry green iguana can hurt a lot!

So even though they don't cost a lot as babies and are neat to look at, don't get a green iguana until you can give it lots of room and the care it needs to be healthy.

For people with a lot of space and a willingness to provide the right type of care, these lizards become like family members (quite different from the green iguanas in their "home-towns," which have been known to be eaten by people).

Green iguana

Chameleons

The green anole I mentioned in chapter 6 is sometimes called a chameleon, but it isn't one. The anole is called this only because it can change color, a trait that it does share with the true chameleons. True chameleons, most originally from Africa and Madagascar, are the lizards with the weird cone-shaped eyes that can move in two different directions at the same time. They are often dazzling to look at, exhibiting blazing colors such as red, turquoise, blue, and yellow. They can change pattern and color very quickly, and this takes place for camouflage purposes, as well as to reflect health and mood. Chameleons have funny-looking feet, with two claws on each foot, and curly tails. They are arboreal lizards, meaning they live in trees and bushes where they move very slowly, walking along branches and among leaves.

Chameleons are considered more delicate than other lizards. These lizards don't do

This is a panther chameleon—can you say "colorful"?

well if they're stressed at all, and many things, including other chameleons, can stress them out. Many chameleons are being bred in captivity, though, and these chameleons are sturdier than the wild-caught ones have been in the past. Still, because of their easily stressed natures and strict care requirements, it's best for beginners to stay away from the cool-looking chameleons.

Camouflage Chameleons

The chameleon is a master at camouflage. This lizard can change its colors and pattern to blend in with its surroundings. This may be a reaction to a change in the environment, such as the temperature going up or down. Or a chameleon may develop stress coloration to express that it is mad or scared. Chameleons also change colors as a way to help attract mates.

Can you spot this Namaqua chameleon crawling across the road?

This Jackson's chameleon's body blends in with the green tree leaves. Its horns, which males use to battle each other, resemble branches.

Here's another chameleon taking on the greens and browns of its treetop retreat.

The Antsingy leaf chameleon has a limited ability to change color. But its brownish hues serve it well in its natural habitat—underneath dead leaves on the forest floor.

Monitor Lizards

There are different types of monitor lizards. Although some are dwarf monitors, many can get very big. As with green iguanas, the babies are cute, and they may not always cost very much, but they will grow up to be quite large. For instance, the Komodo monitor I discussed back in chapter 2 starts out as a cute baby lizard yet grows big enough to eat a goat!

There are Nile monitors, Asian water monitors, savannah monitors, emerald tree monitors, black roughneck monitors, and others. Of these, the savannah is sometimes rec- ommended for beginner lizard keepers because it's not as excitable as the other moni- tors. Still, this lizard gets pretty bulky and big (4 feet, 1.2 m, or so), and a big cage will eventu- ally be necessary.

Monitors are known for their hefty appetites. These lizards love to eat, and they seem always to be hungry. The more young ones eat, the faster they grow and the sooner they will need big cages.

Monitor lizards also burn calories quickly because they are often very active lizards. Some, especially the Nile monitor, have a reputation for being biters.

Monitors are neat lizards, but most get quite big and are very hyper. Beginners should avoid the bigger types, but you could try an ackie someday.

Because of their potential for being large and their active lifestyles, it's best to leave the majority of monitors for the experts. After you've become experienced at keeping lizards, I recommend that, if you want to get a monitor, you think about getting one of the dwarf monitor species that are available. One that people like is called an ackie (which is a shorter, easier-to-pronounce nickname based on its scientific name, *Varanus acanthurus*). Dwarf monitors such as ackies are more manageable than the bigger guys, so keep them in mind for later. (The main reason I didn't include them in the previous chapter is because ackies can be expensive—a couple of hundred dollars—compared with the other beginner lizards I mentioned; you should keep some other species first before making the move to monitors.)

Horned Lizards

These are the lizards that I mentioned back in chapter 2 because they can squirt blood from their eyes when they're scared. I mention them here only because some of you who live in desert areas may find wild horned lizards and want to catch them and take them home.

Don't do it! Horned lizards are one of the hardest lizards to keep in captivity. This is because the main food they need is ants, and they would need more than you would be able to provide regularly. They may eat other tiny insects, but horned lizards never thrive in a beginner's lizard terrarium, so leave the interesting horned lizards where you find them—in the wild.

Does this spotted tokay gecko look friendly to you?

Tokay Geckos

The tokay gecko (it's named after a sound it makes: *toe-kay*) is a very interesting-looking lizard. The tokays you see in pet stores are usually a grayish or pale purple color with orange or brown spots. They have big, bulging eyes with vertical pupils (this means the pupil is a slit that goes from top to bottom rather than being round like a human pupil). They can walk on walls, too. They are big geckos and can grow to about 12 inches (30 cm) in length.

Even though they look neat and aren't very expensive, tokay geckos can be touchy and are often ready to bite— and they bite hard! Leave them for the gecko experts, the ones who wear gloves.

Day Geckos

There are several kinds of day geckos. The one you will probably see most often in stores is the giant day gecko, which is a brilliant bright green with red spots on its back. (Some have only a couple of spots; others have more.) Of them all, the giant day gecko is the one a beginner who wants a day gecko could probably try. It's also active during the day, which is unusual for a gecko (most are nocturnal).

Day geckos are docile, can walk on glass, and don't get huge. Many day geckos are a bit delicate and can easily be injured by rough handling. These lizards are best kept as display animals—to look at, not to hold. For these last two reasons,

Giant day geckos are beautiful green lizards with red dots. They do well in tropical vivarium setups that include plants.

I believe they are better left to lizard keepers who have had some previous experience.

Uromastyx

Uromastyx (pronounced your-oh-MAST-ix) are very easygoing desert lizards that have spiny tails; for this reason, they are also known as spiny-tailed lizards. There are several different types that live in areas such as India, Africa, and Asia. Many hobbyists refer to these lizards as uros, for short. Coloration varies among uromastyx species; the Egyptian uro is mostly a tan-colored lizard, whereas the ornate uro is a very colorful lizard with hues of blue, orange, yellow, and other colors and a spectacular spotted pattern. The Mali uromastyx is another spinytail that you may see for sale.

Uromastyx sp.

Of all the uromastyx, the ornate uro is the prettiest.

Baby uromastyx are often for sale in reptile stores and at reptile expos, and they really are neat lizards. But again, these are lizards that don't always do great in a beginner's cage. Not much is known about them, and people are still learning the best ways to keep them healthy in captivity. Maybe once you're an expert keeper of beginner lizards, more will be known about uromastyx, and you can decide then if you want to get one.

Conclusion

As I said, you're going to see lots of neat lizards when you are looking for one to buy. Some, such as the uromastyx, still have a little mystery attached to them and can be a bit more difficult to keep than others. Yet none of the lizards mentioned in this chapter

would make bad pets for people who know how to care for them.

I know I sound like a broken record, but read as much as you can about lizards before you buy one, including all the lizards I've mentioned in this book. Then, with the help of your family and other smart people, you will be able to decide which type of lizard you will be best able to care for and keep alive. Alive and healthy—that's the best kind of lizard pet!

Speaking of healthy lizards, in the next chapter we'll take a look at some common conditions that could cause your lizards to become sick and what you can do to prevent them from causing your pets harm.

Beginners: stick to bearded dragons!

Bearded dragon

CHAPTER 8

Potential Health Problems

I n the Pet Stores section in chapter 3, we discussed some of the things to look for to help you pick out a healthy lizard. Even if you start with a healthy pet, though, your pet will become sick if you don't take proper care of it. It's also possible that you thought you chose a healthy lizard at the store, but it turned out to be sick.

Blue-tongued skink

If your lizard ever gets sick, my main piece of advice is to take it to a veterinarian. If possible, find a veterinarian who special- izes in reptiles. In this chapter, I will describe some common con- ditions. I hope you won't have to deal with any of them.

Sick animals can be unpredictable, so consider handling them with gloves (especially adult green iguanas like this one).

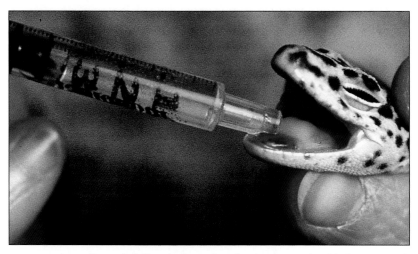

Some people medicate their lizards themselves, but beginners should always consult with a veterinarian if their lizards appear sick.

Metabolic Bone Disease

Known also as nutritional secondary hyperparathyroidism (I know, it's a mouthful), **metabolic bone disease** (MBD) strikes reptiles that are not being cared for properly. The most common cause involves improper levels of calcium, vitamin D₃, and phosphorus.

Green iguanas are the most common victims of MBD, but other lizards can get it, too. Their bones become brittle and deformed, causing the body to become twisted and

Act Fast with Sick Lizards

Sometimes lizards don't show any signs that they're sick until it's too late to save them. This is the result of wild lizard behavior that is still a part of pet lizard behavior. A lizard living in the wild that is obviously sick becomes an easy target for predators and other bullies. It is often killed quickly. This is why lizards don't show signs of illness until they are overcome by it.

The minute you notice your lizard is showing any signs of illness, such as odd patches of skin, a refusal to eat, stuff oozing from its eyes or nose, or a lack of energy, make an appointment to take it to a veterinarian. He or she will conduct tests, and if you're fortunate it won't be too late to save your pet.

Luckily, by practicing good reptile-keeping methods, you can avoid most lizard health problems.

This poor iguana has metabolic bone disease. Note its misshapen jaw; this is a well-known sign that your pet isn't receiving proper care.

knobby. The mouth can appear swollen and bulgy (this is sometimes called rubber jaw). Eventually, the poor lizard becomes crippled and without treatment will die.

If you notice your lizard is beginning to look deformed in any way, is having seizures, or is dragging its legs, get it to a vet right away. It may have MBD.

The good news is that if you take proper care of your lizard, MBD is usually preventable. Giving your lizard suffi-cient calcium, phosphorus, and vitamin D_3 through proper foods and dietary supplements (as mentioned in chapter 5) and providing full-spectrum lighting will go a long way toward preventing MBD.

Internal Parasites

Think of internal parasites as little bugs or worms that can get inside your lizard's body. Once they're in there, they can slowly sap your pet's strength until your pet gets sick. Wild-caught lizards are more likely to have internal parasites than captive-bred ones, but any reptile can pick up parasites.

Usually, you can't tell your lizard has internal parasites until it is actually acting sick, and by then it might be too late to save it. For this reason, it's a good idea to have a **stool** sample (a piece of your lizard's poop) examined by a vet soon after you take your pet home. The vet will inspect it for parasites; if he finds some, he will prescribe some medicine to help get rid of them.

External Parasites

Internal parasites are inside your lizard's body; external parasites are outside, on its skin. External parasites include mites (pictured below) and ticks, two kinds of tiny bugs that can suck a lizard's blood. There are other kinds of external parasites, too, but mites and ticks are the most common. Mites, especially, can attack lizards that are placed into contaminated cages in pet stores and at shipping facilities, where mite-infested lizards have been kept.

Sometimes parasites can invade your lizard's cage, hitch-

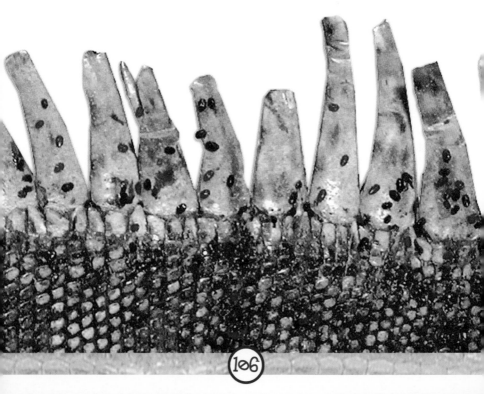

If the vivarium is too dry, your lizard may have trouble shedding its skin properly. A misting with some warm water could help it out.

hiking on a piece of wood you put in the cage or even on some of the live food you may offer your pets. If this happens, you not only have to treat your lizard but also have to completely clean its cage and everything in it.

Even though they can be very small, you can usually see external parasites when they're on your lizard. Mites, for instance, look like teensy red dots that may be clumped together in a fold of skin on your lizard's body. Or you may spy them scurrying around your lizard's body, especially near the eyes and between the scales, or crawling on your hands after handling the lizard. Lizards with mites will sometimes scratch themselves on rocks and branches in their cages.

If you see anything weird on your lizard's skin, take the animal to a vet. External parasites can be removed, and sometimes when a lizard sheds its skin, the parasites are shed along with it, but the longer these beasties are on your pet, the worse it is for the lizard. A vet will help you get rid of them.

Skin-Shedding Problems

Lizards can have problems when they shed their skins. If a lizard doesn't shed its skin completely, the old skin that is left attached can wind around its toes and tighten until the blood flow is cut off. If this isn't taken care of, the toes could eventually fall off!

Like MBD, improper shedding often means that you aren't taking care of your lizard the right way. A common cause is a lack of humidity (moisture) in your lizards' cage. In other words, the cage is too dry too much of the time. Even desert lizards such as bearded dragons need a spraying with water now and then. Humidity helps lizards shed their skins, so if you notice patches of shed skin that are stuck to your lizard, try misting it with warm water sprayed from a water bottle.

It may be tempting to help your lizard shed by tugging off loose pieces of its shedding skin. This isn't always a good idea. If you give a very gentle tug and the skin comes loose, that's usually OK. But don't tug hard if the skin doesn't come away easily because you could end up hurting your pet. Mist with water as recommended, and soon the skin should be easily removed, if it doesn't come off by itself.

If you see nasal discharge, such as this monitor's, or anything oozing from the eyes or mouth, take your lizard to a veterinarian.

Water dragons are known for rubbing their noses raw against the walls of their vivaria, but there are ways you can prevent this from happening (see page 86).

If you try misting your lizard and it still seems to be having problems shedding its skin, your next step is (can you guess what I'm going to say?) to take it to a vet.

Burns and Other Injuries

Every once in a while a lizard burns itself on improperly placed or used heating devices. Hot rocks, for instance, which look like rocks and heat up when they're plugged in (some lizards like to lie on them to keep warm), can sometimes burn a lizard if they malfunction or if their thermostats are set too high. Other times, a lizard may come into contact with a heat lamp and get burned by the bulb.

Because your pet lizards are alive and moving (at least, I

Salmonella

Pet reptiles (mostly turtles) have been linked to cases of *Salmonella* (sal-meh-NEH-lah), but the number of people who get sick from this because of their pet reptiles is small. *Salmonella* is a bacterium that causes a disease called **salmonellosis**, which can make you sick to your stomach, give you diarrhea, and cause other unpleasant side effects. It's most likely to affect kids, senior citizens, and people who have a weak immune system.

The key to avoiding salmonellosis is to keep things clean. Whenever you handle your lizards, wash your hands thoroughly with a disinfectant soap afterward. The same goes for objects used by your reptiles and in their cages such as food and water bowls and cage decorations. Wash them thoroughly, and never handle lizards or their supplies in areas where they could come into contact with your family's food. Don't put your lizards in the sink or the bathtub, either.

Any time you're working with your lizards or any of your lizard-keeping stuff, clean up your work area completely. Don't give *Salmonella* even the teensiest chance to contaminate anything.

hope they are!), they can have accidents. If you carelessly stack rocks in the cage, they could fall onto your pet and hurt it, especially if the lizard is digging beneath the rocks at the time. To avoid this, ask an adult to help you use silicone glue to attach rocks to the bottom of the cage and to each other to prevent them from falling over. If you let your lizard run loose across the living room, one of its toenails could get snagged in the carpeting and accidentally be pulled out when you pick up your pet to return it to its cage.

These are only a couple of examples of possible injuries; others can happen. If your lizard ever has an accident and gets hurt, a vet should examine it and decide on the best type of treatment to get your pet back to tip-top condition.

Impactions

I discussed impactions, also known as intestinal blockages, in chapter 4, in the Substrate section. They can result when a lizard eats its substrate, a piece of food that is too big to pass through its system easily, or the threads and fibers of carpeting and other materials.

An impaction can be deadly if not treated by a veterinarian. To avoid an impaction, inspect your lizard's cage for any potential problems and make changes accordingly. Use digestible sand, for instance, and don't let your lizard loose on any carpeting in your house.

Quarantine

All new lizards should be quarantined before they are placed in a cage with your other lizards. Quarantining keeps new lizards from passing diseases to your healthy lizards. To quarantine a new lizard, keep it in a separate cage for ninety days. Have your vet check it before introducing it to the lizards you already have. One sick lizard placed with several healthy lizards is a bad thing because soon they could all be sick!

CHAPTER 9

Do's and Don'ts for Lizard Owners

The following ten dos and ten don'ts will ensure you get the right lizard for you and will help you take care of it properly. All twenty are covered in more detail elsewhere in this book. I hope that you use them to make your lizard-keeping experiences happy ones and that you and your lizards are together for many years!

Baby water dragons

Always learn everything you can about lizards before you get any for a pet.

Do read a lot and conduct research before buying a lizard.

Do buy healthy lizards.

Do provide a cage large enough for your lizards.

Do install full-spectrum lighting for diurnal lizards.

Do feed your lizards healthy foods that are appropriate for them.

Do give your pet lizards vitamin and mineral supplements.

Do keep your lizard's cage clean.

Do be on the lookout for any signs of illness.

Do take your lizard to a veterinarian when it is sick.

Do remember to always wash your hands after handling your lizard and anything in its cage.

As you can see by this open-mouth display, this shingleback skink is feeling ornery.

Don't buy any lizard on impulse.

Don't buy a lizard without knowing how big it will get.

Don't get a lizard unless you are absolutely sure you can take care of it for as long as it will live.

Don't take home a sick lizard thinking you'll make it well.

Don't just stick a lizard in a cage and expect it to thrive without the proper care.

Don't feed herbivorous lizards only iceberg lettuce.

Don't litter or leave logs and rocks overturned when looking for lizards in nature. Leave things as you find them.

Don't let your lizards run loose around your house.

Don't keep more than one male lizard of the same type in the same cage.

Don't delay in taking your lizard to a vet if it is sick.

And last but not least, here's one never:
Never *stop learning about lizards!*

Glossary

arboreal: living in trees

autotomy: a defense mechanism that allows part of an animal's body to break off (lizards drop their tails)

basking: lying in the sun (or in a cage, lying in a heated area) to warm up

camouflage: to hide or disguise oneself, as a chameleon does when it changes colors to blend in with its environment

captive-bred: a reptile that is born from parents kept in captivity

captivity: kept in a cage to prevent escape; living in captivity is the opposite of living in the wild or in nature

carnivorous: meat-eating

cold-blooded: having a body temperature that goes up or down with the temperature of the environment; an ectotherm

crest: a growth on an animal's head that stands out and may be colorful

defense mechanism: a natural behavior that an animal uses to defend itself when it is scared

diurnal: active during the day

dusting: coating insects with a vitamin-mineral supplement powder before feeding them to a reptile

ectotherm: a cold-blooded animal

endangered: an animal with only a small number of its kind left in the wild

gut load: to feed insects nutritious foods before feeding them to a reptile as a way to make sure the reptile gets an extra healthy diet

habitat: the specific area in which an animal naturally lives

herbivorous: plant-eating

herp: a nickname for a reptile; comes from herpetology, the study of reptiles and amphibians

herping: a word hobbyists use to describe looking for reptiles in nature

hibernate: to be in a resting state in which there is almost no activity

hobbyist: a person who keeps reptiles as pets and studies them for fun

insectivorous: insect-eating

larval: refers to the early part of an animal's life when the appearance of the hatchling is very different than the appearance of the adult; a caterpillar, for example, is a butterfly or moth larva

metabolic bone disease (MBD): a disease usually caused by a lack of calcium in the diet, which results in weak, deformed bones

morph: an animal with a special color or pattern

nocturnal: active at night

omnivorous: plant- and meat-eating

pinky mice (pinkies): newborn mice that get this nickname because their hairless bodies are pink

range: the area of a country (or even specific parts of a region or state) that a reptile can be found in the wild

regeneration: the process of growing back a body part (such as a lizard's tail) that broke off as a defense mechanism or because of an injury

reptile: an animal from the class Reptilia, a group of cold-blooded, air-breathing animals that move on their bellies or on short legs (such as snakes, lizards, and turtles) and have skin covered with scales or bony plates

salmonellosis: a disease caused by *Salmonella* bacteria that humans can catch from reptiles; symptoms include upset stomach and diarrhea in humans

stool: poop

substrate: the material you put on the bottom of a reptile's cage

thermal gradient: the temperature range you create by placing heating elements only on one side of the cage; allows the cold-blooded reptile to move either to the warm side or cool side of the cage to reach its desired body temperature

thermoregulation: the changing of body temperature by moving from a warm place to a cool place, or from a cool place to a warm place

thermostat: a device attached to a heating element that you can set to maintain a specific temperature

ultraviolet (UV) light: a type of light that humans can't see

veterinarian (vet): an animal doctor

vivarium: a cage used to house reptiles, amphibians, and sometimes insects; similar to a terrarium

wild-caught: captured in the wild

Recommended Reading

Reptiles Magazine
A monthly publication covering herps from A to Z.
The Web site provides useful care tips as well as links
to breeders, photo galleries, and message boards.
http://www.reptilesmagazine.com
PO Box 6050
Mission Viejo, CA 92690

The following two field guides have been around for many years
and are still favorites of many herpers in the United States. Both
are available in paperback and are part of the popular Peterson
Field Guides series.

Conant, Roger and Joseph Collins. *A Field Guide to Reptiles and
Amphibians: Eastern and Central North America.* 4th ed. Houghton
Mifflin, 1998.

Stebbins, Robert. *A Field Guide to Western Reptiles.* 3rd ed.
Houghton Mifflin, 2003.

About the Author

Russ Case is the editor of the monthly magazines *Reptiles*, *Aquarium Fish Magazine*, and *Freshwater and Marine Aquarium magazine*, as well as the annual magazines *Reptiles USA*, *Aquarium USA*, and *Marine Fish and Reef USA*. He lives in Southern California and has been a reptile and amphibian enthusiast since he was a small child exploring the wilds of suburban New Jersey in the 1960s. Lizards are his favorite herps, but he's also very fond of snakes, turtles, and amphibians, and he has kept many different types over the years. He is shown here holding the only two venomous lizard species in the world: the beaded lizard (the big one) and the Gila monster (smaller, on top of the beaded). Neither one bit him.

Photo Credits

COVER
Front cover (main image): Bill Love; (top box): Gerold Merker;
(top middle box): Paul Freed; (bottom middle and bottom boxes): David Northcott.

FRONT MATTER
Title and Contents: Paul Freed.

CHAPTER 1
4, 5 (top), 8: David Northcott. 5 (bottom): Paul Freed. 6: Gerold Merker.
7: Photos.com. 9: Lindsay Pike.

CHAPTER 2
10: Gerold Merker. 11 (top): Photos.com. 11 (bottom), 12 (#1, 2, and 3), 13 (top and
middle), 15, 17 (box), 18, 21 (bottom), 22 (bottom left), 23: Paul Freed. 12 (#4),
13 (bottom), 16, 17, 21 (top), 22 (bottom right): David Northcott. 14: Bill Love.
19: Lindsay Pike. 22 (top): James Gerholdt.

CHAPTER 3
24, 35 (box only), 36 (bottom left), 41 (computer monitor): Photos.com. 25, 28, 34
(top), 36 (bottom right), 37 (bottom), 38: David Northcott. 26 (top), 29, 30, 31:
Shutterstock.com. 26 (bottom), 27, 32–33, 34 (bottom), 36 (top), 37 (top),
41 (lizard): Paul Freed. 35 (lizard): © 2001 PhotoDisc, Inc. 39, 40: Julie Bergman.

CHAPTER 4
42, 56 (lizard), 58: David Northcott. 43 (top), 44–46, 47 (top middle and bottom middle),
49 (top), 50–51, 53–55, 57 (lizard): Paul Freed. 43 (bottom), 47 (bottom),
49 (bottom): Phillipe de Vosjoli. 47 (top): James Gerholdt. 52: Lindsay Pike.
56–57 (art supplies): Photos.com. 57 (top): Paul Freed. 59: Julie Bergman.

CHAPTER 5
60, 61 (bottom), 62, 63 (bottom), 66–70: Paul Freed. 61 (top): David Northcott.
63, 65: Maleta M. Walls.

CHAPTER 6
72, 73 (bottom), 76 (top), 86, 89: David Northcott. 73 (top), 74–75, 78–79, 81–82, 84,
87–88: Paul Freed. 76 (bottom), 80, 90: © 2001 PhotoDisc, Inc. 77, 91: Phillipe de Vosjoli.

CHAPTER 7
92–93, 95, 96 (top and bottom), 98–99, 100 (top): Paul Freed. 94, 101 (bottom): David
Northcott. 96 (top middle and bottom middle), 97: Photos.com. 100 (bottom),
101 (top): Lindsay Pike.

CHAPTER 8
102, 105: David Northcott. 103 (top), 110: Photos.com. 103 (bottom),
104, 106: Roger Klingenberg. 107–109: Paul Freed.

CHAPTER 9
112–114: Paul Freed.

GLOSSARY
115: Bill Love. 116: Paul Freed. 117 (top): David Northcott. 117 (bottom): © 2001
PhotoDisc, Inc.

ABOUT THE AUTHOR
119: Russ Case.

Stickers illustrated by Tom Kimball.

Lizard Stickers

Can you find where to place these in the book?

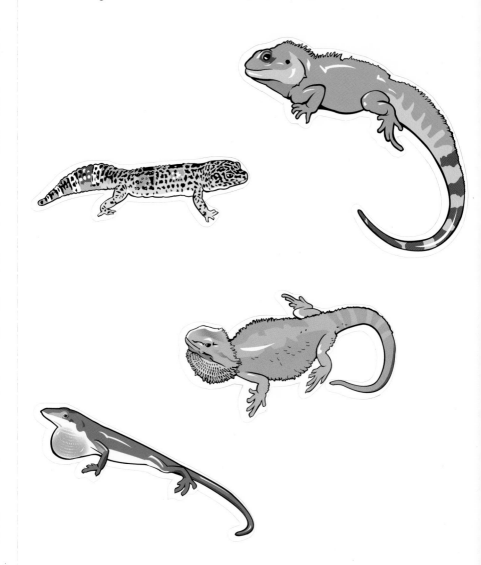